PerryScope

2

Articles at random dates
2016-2017

Perry Diaz

Published by

TATAY JOBO ELIZES.
Self-Publisher
in 2017, under the
permission and authorization
of PERRY DIAZ,
author and owner of the copyright to this book. The copyright owner can withdraw this permission at his discretion without any objection from Talay Jobo Elizes at any time. Printing of this book is using the present day method of Print-On-Demand (POD) system, where prints will never run out of copies to be available for posterity. The copyright owner is free to republish with other publishers anytime.

ISBN - 13: 978 - 1977664914
ISBN - 10: 1977664911

Contact: job_elizes@yahoo.com
Website: http://tinyurl.com/mj76ccq

Special Note

*Articles are arranged at
random dates in 2016-2017*

Contents

About the author – *p4*

1 - Digong's "neutral" foreign policy
    February 15, 2017 – p6

2 - Are Duterte and Trump the new normal?
    November 18, 2016 – p13

3 - Duterte's Flip-Flop Diplomacy
    November 2, 2016 – p20

4 - Did China Trick Digong?
    November 7, 2016 – p27

5 - Digong was the 'Manchurian Candidate'
    all Along! - October 24, 2016 – p34

6 - Beware the Ides of October –
    October 16, 2016 – p41

7 - A Nation in Pain - Oct. 11, 2016 – p49

8 - 'Strategic Diamond' takes shape in the
    Pacific - September 8, 2016 – p57

9 - Foreign Policy Fiasco
    September 19, 2016 – p65

10 - China Sets Eyes on Benham Rise
    September 27, 2016 – p72

**11 - The Philippines at a dangerous
  Crossroads - October 3, 2016 – p79**

**12 - The Philippines' three historical mistake
  Sept. 11, 2016 – p85**

**13 - Duterte's Honeymoon with China
  May 30, 2016 – p93**

**14 – Duterte's brand of politics
  May 24, 2016 – p101**

**15 - Duterte: Strongman With A Soft Spot
  May 16, 2016 – p108**

**15 - Why I Publish/Reprint Books
  Tatay Jobo Elizes - p115**

ooooo

About the Author

Perry Diaz started publishing Balita (Global) as a community newsletter in 1987. Over the years, his commentaries and viewpoints have become increasingly popular with Pinoys in the United States, Philippines and abroad. In 2003, Perry started publishing his opinion articles by the name of Perryscope. Today, Global Balita is a daily-published online culmination of Perryscopes, social commentaries, news and features from a variety of respected sources about Filipinos and all that affect them.

All articles can be read freely online at his website PerryScopes or Global Balita, easily accessible in the internet. Also at WFA yahoogp.

The articles are being archived in printed or hardcopy for posterity under print-on-demand system so that prints will never run out. This will serve all readers, young and old, internet-savvy or not, Filipinos or not, for all generations to come.

Affiliations: Member of the Sheriff's Community Advisory Board, Sacramento; Moderator, FilAm Media; Community Advisory Panel Member, Sacramento Municipal Utility District; Member of and Cal Expo Board, Sacramento County; Founding Member, The Filipino Journal; Founder, GlobalBalita.com; Education, Bachelor of Science Industrial Engineering, Adamson University.)

Visit www.GlobalBalita.com for more news and updates.

To contact Perry Diaz directly, please email perrydiaz@gmail.com.
For advertising opportunities, please email globalbalita@gmail.com.

1
Digong's "neutral" foreign policy

February 15, 2017

President Rodrigo "Digong" Duterte made a big splash in the international scene by declaring that he was pursuing an "independent" foreign policy. Then he declared his "separation" from the U.S.; threatened to terminate military treaties with the U.S. and proposed defense alliance with China and Russia. The world leaders did not bat an eye. But when his campaign against drug lords turned bloody – more than 3,000 drug pushers and users in less than 60 days – U.S. President Barack Obama indicated some concerns. Digong didn't take it too well and called Obama "son of a whore." Obama nonchalantly ignored him, saying: *"I have seen some of those colorful statements in the past. Clearly he's a colorful guy."*

But the newly inaugurated U.S. President Donald J. Trump took a different tact. He called Digong while he was still president-elect and they talked for several minutes. He praised Digong on his campaign against illegal drugs, saying he was doing it the "right way."

There seems to be great expectations from a Trump presidency, which could give U.S.-Philippines relations some room for "reconciliation" particularly now that Obama has left office.

On the international scene, expect a great deal of geopolitical movements in an emerging multi-polar world order with the U.S., Russia, and China competing for dominance in world affairs.

Sino-American conflict

While Trump seems comfortable with Russian President Vladimir Putin, he has irked Chinese President Xi Jinping when Trump questioned the "One-China" policy that has maintained U.S.-China relations on an even keel for the past four decades. Trump made it known that he is not committed to the "One-China" policy. "Everything is under negotiation, including One-China," he said. Beijing angrily responded, saying that the "One-China" policy is "non-negotiable."

Trump also accused China of currency manipulation and unfair trade practices. In addition, he questioned China's reclamation of seven reefs in the South China Sea and building militarized artificial islands around them.

With the Senate expected to confirm Trump's nomination of Rex "T-Rex" Tillerson as Secretary of State, the situation in the South China Sea could spiral into a war between the U.S. and China. During his Senate confirmation hearing, Tillerson likened China's illegal occupation of several reefs in the Spratly archipelago to Russia's annexation of Crimea. He said that the White House needed to send China a "clear signal" that such activities had to stop. He also said that the U.S. would defend "international territories" in the strategic waterway and block China's access to these islands.

Tillerson's blunt warnings and proposed actions did not dwell too well with Beijing who told Washington to tread carefully "to avoid harming the peace and stability of the South China Sea." Declaring that China has "irrefutable" sovereignty – China used the term "indisputable" before – over the disputed islands, China's state-owned media warned that any attempt to prevent China from accessing her interests in the region would risk sparking a "large-scale war." Interestingly, China had already deployed "significant" weapons systems, including anti-aircraft and anti-missile system, on these islands.

U.S.-Philippines alliance

Meanwhile, the newly Senate-confirmed Secretary of Defense, Gen. James "Mad Dog" Mattis, will be going on a three-day visit to Japan and South Korea on February 1 to reassure them of Washington's commitment to the security of the volatile Asia-Pacific. There are 28,500 American troops in South Korea and 50,000 in Japan.

But while Japan and South Korea welcomed the deployment of U.S. forces to their countries, the Philippines was wary of American presence in the Philippines, which has three defense agreements with the U.S., including a Mutual Defense Treaty. President Duterte whose hatred of the U.S. has led him to distance from the U.S. and got closer to China and Russia, wants to get rid of all foreign troops out of the country within two years and that he was willing to revoke base-hosting agreements with the U.S.

Last January 26, the Philippines' Defense Secretary Gen. Delfin Lorenzana – concerned that the Philippines will be caught in the middle of a U.S.-China conflict in the south China Sea – said in a press briefing, *"I'm waiting for my counterpart, Secretary Mattis. I'd like to talk to him to get his sense about these [security] policies because he will be the one to implement that."*

Then he said something that was never mentioned before: The Philippines should "maintain neutrality in its foreign policy." Huh?

Neutrality and mutual defense

Lorenzana said, *"We are very wary. Let's see. We will think very hard if it will be implemented by the US, those pronouncements that they will prevent the Chinese from retaining these islands. We will react accordingly when the time comes, when they will start to do that… We might be caught in the middle."* Then he added, *"In the first place, how can they [Chinese] prevent them [Americans] from going there? They [Americans] are already there…. We will have to discuss with the National Security Council if and when the Americans will really come to the South China Sea and implement those pronouncements."* There is not much that the

Philippines could do to stop a U.S.-China conflict in the South China Sea. However, if war breaks out between the U.S. and China, the U.S. could invoke the Mutual Defense Treaty (MDT) and the Philippines would be expected to come to her aid. And this was what Lorenzana was trying to avoid when he mentioned a "neutral" foreign policy.

But in a press conference on January 27, Lorenzana said the U.S.-Philippines Enhanced Defense Cooperation Agreement (EDCA), which allows American troops to build facilities in Philippine military bases – is "still on."

"According to the Pentagon, they will start constructing some facilities in the EDCA chosen camps… Basa Air Base, Bautista Air Base in Palawan… I think the first they will develop is Basa… with a runway and put up facilities also for their troops. Mga imbakan nila ng mga gamit nila kung nandito sila [It will be a storage for their equipment here]," Lorenzana said, adding the American troops could come back anytime should they decide to leave. He also said construction of facilities may start anytime as construction costs were already included in the U.S. fiscal year of 2017.

Lorenzana also reportedly said, *"Aside from Cooperation Afloat Readiness and Training (CARAT) and Philippines-U.S. Amphibious Landing Exercise (PHIBLEX), other military exercises with the U.S. troops will continue."*

Now, that's a total turnaround in just a day – from pursuing a "neutral" foreign policy to total commitment to implementing EDCA and continuing with joint military exercises, particularly the Balikatan or shoulder-to-shoulder joint exercises.

Which makes one wonder: Did Trump call Digong secretly in the middle of the night reassuring him of Uncle Sam's commitment to the security of the Philippines? Or was it just a "guni-guni" (imagination) during one of Digong's sleepless nights? Or did Japanese Prime Minister Shinzo Abe make good of his pledge of $6.88 billion aid package when they had breakfast at Digong's private residence in Davao City? And didn't Abe and Digong agree that the Philippines, Japan, and the United States would work cooperatively together? That's a lot of questions but the answers are clearly manifested in recent geopolitical movements that translate favorably to the mutual benefit of the Philippines and America. Isn't that what "mutual defense" is all about?

The bottom line is: "Neutrality" and "mutual defense" are mutually exclusive. They cannot be applied together; it's either one or the other. If Digong wants to pursue a "neutral" foreign policy, he has to terminate all defense agreements with the U.S. and start buying warships, submarines, and fighter jets for the defense of the Philippines.

Ooooo

2
Are Duterte and Trump the new normal?
November 18, 2016

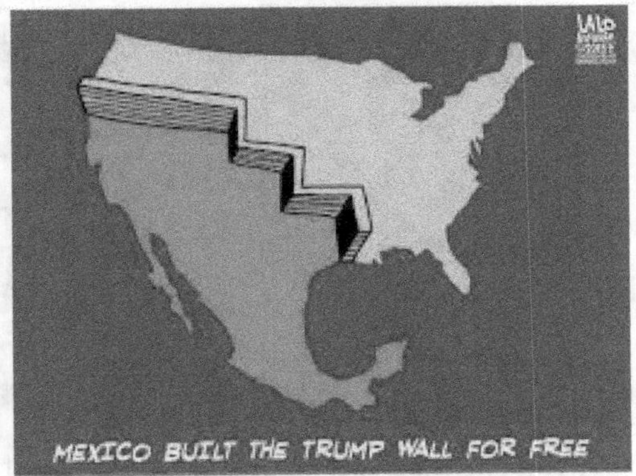

The "Wall" at the U.S.-Mexico border proposed by Trump.

The election of Rodrigo R. Duterte and Donald J. Trump — six months apart – as president of the Philippines and United States, respectively, shook the world in a manner that differed from previous presidential elections in both countries. While Duterte was favored to win in large part due to his promise to kill drug pushers and users, Trump was doomed to lose simply because of his controversial stand against a lot of issues and causes that many people consider as "sacred cows." But as it turned out, the "sacred cows" were as fair game as anything else, which — surprisingly – had attracted the support of many Americans. "I'll build the wall and tell Mexico to pay for it," Trump promised, and his supporters went a-gaga!

It's the same thing with Duterte who told his supporters at a campaign rally: "I'll kill 100,000 drug pushers and users and throw their bodies into the Manila Bay to fatten the fishes." And his supporters went bananas!

Yes, it's indeed a world gone crazy! What the hell happened? But the question should be: "What happened in hell?" And hell is what *hoi polloi* think of the environment they're living in today, which reminds me of Dan Brown's book, *"Inferno."* A character, *Dr. Brooks,* who was visiting Manila said, *"I've run through the gates of hell,"* to describe the crime, poverty, and sex trade that she saw.

And for all the hellish situations that the people have to coup with, they can only blame their governments for not doing enough to make their lives worth living. And all the politicians running for office in both countries – two of the freest democracies on earth – know it. Duterte and Trump saw an opportunity to get ahead of the crowded pack of presidential wannabes by inflaming the emotions of the people. While some people laughed them off, a growing number of people began to wonder, "Why not?"

Duterte made "War on Drugs" the cornerstone of his campaign for the presidency. And true enough he delivered. During his first 100 days in office, more than 4,000 drug pushers and users ended up dead on the streets. The police said that the police gunned down 1,200 of them when they resisted arrest. The rest were tagged as "death under investigation" (DUI), a newly coined term for someone killed under mysterious circumstances, mostly by vigilantes.

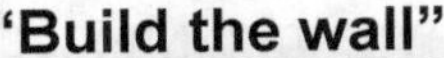

"Build the wall"

Meanwhile, as Trump savored his stunning victory over Hillary Clinton who won the popular vote — which doesn't count — but lost the electoral vote to Trump, a lot of Americans wonder how Trump would craft his domestic programs and foreign policy, after all those nasty things that he said about certain groups of Americans and America's allies as well.

If there is one scorching issue that has ignited emotional backlash from Trump's supporters, it's "illegal immigration." With an estimated 11 million illegals residing in the U.S., Trump's solution to this problem is two-fold. First, deport the illegals. And second, build a wall to prevent them from entering the U.S. by way of the porous U.S.-Mexico border. Then he inflamed his supporters' emotion when he accused the Mexican government of sending criminals, rapists, drug pushers, and other undesirable across the border. He promised that the Mexican government would pay for the wall's construction. The question is: Is Mexico willing to pay for the wall?

But regardless of whether Mexico would pay for the wall or not, the perceived "danger" of undesirable aliens crossing the border in record numbers has already been ingrained in the minds of his supporters. In other words, Trump stoked xenophobic fear of Mexican illegal immigrants, which he considers as a threat to national security.

Geopolitics is addition

Duterte, Xi, Putin: The new triumvirate?

If there is one major and critical area of concern among geopolitical experts, it's foreign policy. Duterte made headlines during his state visit to China last October when he declared that he was pursuing an "independent foreign policy." He also announced his "separation" from the U.S., which caused a geopolitical tremor of tectonic proportion, which left the Philippines' allies — particularly the U.S. – trembling. And to drive his point, he said that he would seek economic and military alliance with China and Russia.

Duterte's flirting with China and Russia is nothing more than "puppy love." But what truly caused a lot of headaches among America's allies were Trump's threats to withdraw American forces from Japan and South Korea unless they pay the cost of their deployment in their countries. He also made similar threats to America's NATO allies and even suggested that NATO disbands, which made Russian President Vladimir Putin happier than Dr. Strangelove fiddling with the Doomsday Machine.

But in the event that Duterte and Trump find solace to the notion that foreign policy is not zero-sum game but an intricate art of "geopolitics is addition," they just might play down their rhetoric and do what is best for their people. Let me put it this way: Duterte will need America more than China and Russia combined, while Trump needs NATO as a counterforce to Russian expansion. He also needs America's treaty allies Japan, South Korea, Australia, Philippines, Thailand, and Taiwan to contain China and North Korea.

But there is a silver lining to all the gloom and doom that Trump has been trumpeting around; he wants to make the U.S. stronger to maintain the balance of power in a world in turmoil. During the final days of this year's presidential elections, Trump laid out an ambitious plan to build 350 new warships for the U.S. Navy to match the growing navies of China and Russia.

Ideological shift

Who will Trump nominate to take the late Justice Antonin Scalia's seat?

But the most significant aspect of Duterte and Trump's elections is that both of them will have the opportunity to change the ideological make-up of their respective country's Supreme Court. In the case of Duterte, he'd be appointing 11 new Supreme Court Justices to replace justices who will be retiring when they reach the mandatory retirement age of 70. With only four justices left from the current bench, Duterte – who is an avowed leftist – would presumably appoint justices in his own image.

In the case of the U.S. Supreme Court where there is no mandatory retirement age, Trump will surely nominate a hard-core conservative to take the seat of the late ultraconservative Justice Antonin Scalia; thus, maintaining the conservative majority on the High Court. However, Justice Anthony Kennedy, although considered a conservative, had oftentimes held the swing vote in big cases; thus, giving the liberals a tactical edge over the conservatives. Another swing vote is Chief Justice John Roberts, who wrote the majority opinion in favor of Obamacare to the chagrin of his fellow conservatives.

However, the shaky equilibrium on the High Court might tilt to the conservative side if one or two of the four liberals' seats were vacated. Among the conservatives, Justice Kennedy at 80 is the oldest. If his seat is vacated, Trump would nominate an ideological conservative to take his seat; thus, solidly strengthening the conservative bloc on the Supreme Court.

With Duterte exiting in six years and Trump in four or eight years, both would leave a lasting legacy that would determine the future of their respective countries. Duterte would leave a left-leaning Supreme Court while Trump would leave the most conservative Supreme Court for the last 50 years, if not the last century.

At the end of the day, what we're seeing is that unorthodoxy has become an acceptable behavior among our political leaders. Duterte and Trump's campaign styles have led people to call Duterte the Trump of the Philippines and Trump as the Duterte of the U.S. Their opponents have called them "loose cannons." But loose cannons or not, they're now the leaders of their countries, which begs the question: Are Duterte and Trump the new normal?

Ooooo

3
Duterte's Flip-Flop Diplomacy
November 2, 2016

When President Rodrigo "Digong" Duterte announced his "separation" from the United States during his state visit to China, it shook the world. Not that it would have changed the balance of power in the Indo-Asia-Pacific region, but it was because of the abrupt – "strange," I might say – way of which it was announced. But what is surreally baffling is his retraction the next day. Is it a case of Dr. Jekyll and Mr. Hyde syndrome or it's just plain grandstanding?

One personality wants to maintain the status quo on U.S.-Philippine relations while the other personality wants to sever all ties with the U.S. and align with the "ideological flow" of China and Russia. And in a moment of Napoleonic illusion, he saw himself as part of an alliance – China, Philippines, and Russia — against the world! Why didn't he include North Korea?

The problem is: Duterte (also known as Du30) seems to live in his own little world totally detached from the geopolitical realities that dictate how nations – and their leaders — interact with one another. He seems to think of the Philippines as an island onto itself that can provide security for her people without help from anybody. And, worst, dismantling the Philippines' military ties with the U.S. would strip the Philippines of the capability to defend her sovereignty and territorial integrity.

Digong's brand of geopolitics

Duterte, Xi, and Putin.

Evidently, Duterte's brand of geopolitics digresses from established norms and conventions in international relations. His handling of the Philippines' West Philippine Sea/South China Sea claims vis-à-vis the Permanent Court of Arbitration's (PCA) ruling, which is overwhelmingly favorable to the Philippines, has bungled the country's strong case against China. Had Duterte stayed on course in pursuing the Philippines' claims, the other claimant-countries could have used the PCA ruling to pursue their own maritime claims against China.

It's interesting to note that with all the geopolitical mishaps and diplomatic faux pas that Duterte did, he had the temerity to claim that he was a Foreign Service graduate. At a press conference last October 19 during his state visit to China, Filipino journalist Ellen Tordesillas quoted him in her column as saying: *"Now that I am the President, by the grace of God, I read a lot; I'm a lawyer and I studied geopolitics and all, and also I am a graduate of the Foreign Service so I get to know how to balance this contending (forces)."*

But what Digong did was break one of the rules of geopolitics, which is: *"Geopolitics is not a zero-sum game."* Indeed, in today's globalized economy, the object of geopolitics is to arrive at a win-win situation where players need to compromise. Gone are the days when nations go to war to settle territorial disputes. The Cold War is over and we are now living in a multipolar world order where all nations are interdependent with one another. The world is shrinking too; and everybody is just a "click" away.

Philippine President Rodrigo Duterte, center, accompanied by Transportation Secretary Arthur Tugade, right, and Defense Secretary Delfin Lorenzana, left, clap their hands at the end of Japan's coast guard drills in Yokohama, Oct. 27, 2016.

Digong's attempted maneuver to "separate" from the U.S. — militarily and economically — and threatened to form an alliance with China and Russia, did not only fail to materialize but it also made a "village clown" of himself. And while he made all these geopolitical and diplomatic boo-boos, his Foreign Secretary Perfecto Yasay Jr. and Defense Secretary Delfin Lorenzana had the thankless job of straightening out the knots and kinks of his "independent foreign policy," which has been causing a lot of embarrassment for him.

It's all drama

With all the "Du30 drama" he staged in Beijing, Duterte was able to attract $24 billion in investments and loans from China. It must have made Chinese President Xi Jinping feel triumphant that the Philippines — under Duterte's leadership – is now in his pocket, totally detached from the U.S. And it would certainly have given him a firm grip on the vast South China Sea. Wrong!

The day Digong returned to the Philippines, he clarified that he's not cutting ties with the U.S. He said he was just pursuing a "separation of foreign policy" from the U.S., which was quite different in meaning and purpose to what he proclaimed in China, which was "separation from the U.S." He said that he didn't want it to affect local jobs in American-owned companies in the Philippines and the large number of Filipinos in the U.S. He also said that it is in the best interest of the Philippines to maintain diplomatic relations with the U.S.

Volte face

An article on the *Nikkei Asian Review* titled, **"Duterte's 'about-face' unsettles Xi,"** published last October 28, talked about Duterte's *volte face* [an act of turning around so as to face in the opposite direction] upon his return to the Philippines. The report said: *"The Internet was not slow to react to Duterte's volte face, and the word 'fraud' has gone viral. One social media post read, 'Duterte changed his face as soon as he returned to the Philippines after securing money from China.'*

"The reference was to the traditional Chinese art of 'face changing,' where performers go from one character to the next by swapping masks in a Beijing opera or during a banquet.

Many feel it was not the mask that was changed so much as a complete change of heart.

"Other online posts put it in less uncertain terms, 'China got dumped. China was deceived,' read one. Another said, 'It is a divorce in disguise [from the U.S.] for the sake of borrowing [from China]. That's not uncommon in China.'"

Damage control

Foreign Secretary Perfecto Yasay Jr. informed Romualdez of his appointment yesterday at the Imperial Tower Hotel in Tokyo, on the sidelines of Duterte's three-day official visit.

It must have occurred to Duterte that he didn't have to let go of the U.S. now that he had secured a huge economic package from China. During his subsequent visit to Japan following the China trip, he appointed *Philippine Star* columnist Babe Romualdez as special envoy to the U.S., reportedly as part of a "rebooting" of relationship with the U.S.

The *Philippine Star* report said: *"Foreign Secretary Perfecto Yasay Jr. informed Romualdez of his appointment yesterday at the Imperial Tower Hotel in Tokyo, on the sidelines of Duterte's three-day official visit.*

" 'We are trying on how we can work with the changes… especially with the upcoming

elections in the US so we will see how we can (establish)… let's call it as rebooting our relationship with the US,' said a member of the President's official delegation here.

" 'We'd like to communicate the message of how we will have a rebooting of our relationship,' the official, who declined to be named, added. 'Yes, of course we will continue our relationship with the US.'

"As special envoy, Romualdez's 'special mission' is to put back on track Philippine-US relations," the report concluded, which begs the question: Can Romualdez fix the damage Digong made?

Geopolitics is addition

Duterte and U.S. Secretary of State John Kerry.

Now that Digong has his cake, he wants to eat it, too. But while a zero-sum game might produce intermediate success in the short term, just like what Digong did on his China visit; he should – nay, must! — realize that in the long term, good geopolitics produces better results if it weren't played as a zero-sum game. It reminds me of the late legendary political leader Eulogio "Amang" Rodriguez whose mantra was "Politics is addition." And so is Geopolitics.

At the end of the day, Digong's flip-flop diplomacy may have worked in his favor at this time, but he must be careful because it could boomerang the next time he flip-flops.

ooooo

4
Did China Trick Digong?
Nov. 7, 2016

When President Rodrigo "Digong" Duterte was sworn in last June 30, 2016, the first person he introduced to the audience was former President Fidel V. Ramos, whom he credited for helping him launch his presidential candidacy. It did not then come as a surprise when Digong appointed Ramos as his special envoy to China.

Immediately, Ramos went to Hong Kong to make contact with a former high-ranking Chinese official and a few other Chinese personalities to "break the ice." But as Ramos had told reporters upon his return to Manila, "It's not really a breakthrough in a sense that there is no ice here in Hong Kong to break but the fish we eat… are cooked in delicious recipes."

After that, Duterte's people started making arrangements for his China trip. They even had a date set for the visit – October 18-21. But the official invitation did not come until the last minute. With an entourage of more than 400 business people, cabinet members, presidential aides, generals, journalists, and kibitzers, Digong flew into the red dragon's lair. After four days of bad-mouthing the Americans, he brought home $24 billion in investment pledges and loans, including $13.5 billion in trade deals. The question is: what concession did he give the Chinese?

But no sooner had Digong landed in Manila than he pivoted 180 degrees and reaffirmed U.S.-Philippine ties. Given his avowed dislike – or to be more precise, hatred of the U.S. – why would he make a fool of himself with such diplomatic boo-boos and flip-flops? Or, as Americans love to say, "Are you out of your mind?"`

Dangerous game

Well, Duterte is not out of his mind but what appeared to have happened was he was playing China and the U.S. off each other, perhaps hoping to get the best of both worlds. But what he didn't realize was that he was dealing with pros. China is the second biggest economic power next to the U.S. and for a third-world country to play China against the U.S. – the Philippines' treaty ally – is something that's not in the playbook of geopolitics. Nobody has done that and succeeded in getting concessions from both sides. On the contrary, Digong might find himself caught in a vise because China and the U.S. are big trading partners with interlocking economic interests. So, when push comes to shove, the two superpowers could – or would – find ways to amicably settle their differences and throw Digong under the bus.

What China wants

Nine-dash line

But ultimately, China would try to get what she had always wanted – sovereignty over the South China Sea (SCS), which includes all the islands, rocks, reefs, and shoals in these waters. And also all the marine resources, and oil and gas deposits, which would provide China with food and energy for her 1.4 billion people. Thus, there is just no way that China would give away any part of the SCS without going to war, which

Duterte already conceded when he said, "We cannot win a war with China." However, Senior Associate Justice Antonio Carpio said at the closing ceremony of the 33rd Philippines-U.S. Amphibious Landing Exercise (Phiblex) last October 12, "There is only one power on earth that can stop the Chinese and that's the U.S." Digong knows that. And the Chinese know it, too. They also know that the Philippines a geostrategic buffer zone that the U.S. can use to counter China and prevent her from breaking out into the Second Island Chain in the Western Pacific, America's last line of defense.

With five Philippine military bases that the Americans can use to deploy their forces, it would be too much of a risk for China to start a war in the SCS. However, if war breaks out, the Philippines will be on the front-line, which is just around 100 miles from the Spratly archipelago where China had built seven militarized artificial islands. Then there are the U.S. bases in Japan, South Korea, Australia, and Singapore. And with five aircraft carrier battle groups under the joint command of the 3rd Fleet and 7th Fleet and a fleet of nuclear ballistic missile submarines, the U.S. would have more than sufficient forces to maintain peace and stability in the Indo-Asia-Pacific Region… and keep China at bay.

Quid pro quo

President Duterte cozying up to Chinese Ambassador to the Philippines Zhao Jianhua.

Although Ramos was credited for "breaking the ice" in China-Philippine relations, what really paved the way for Digong's celebrated state visit to China were Sen. Alan Peter Cayetano and Transportation Secretary Arthur Tugade's "unpublicized" – or secret – trip to China last June prior to Duterte's inauguration. U.S. Ambassador Philip Goldberg revealed this when he was recently interviewed at the ANC talk show, "Headstart." The question is: Did Cayetano and Tugade strike a "quid pro quo" deal with the Chinese?

Someone who may have played a key role in forging the Chinese-Philippine connection was Chinese Ambassador to the Philippines Zhao Jianhua. The groundwork for this "connection" may have been laid out when Zhao and several Chinese businessmen visited then president-elect Duterte in Davao City. Zhao, who had kept a low profile during former President Aquino's time, has been a "frequent visitor" to Davao City and Malacanang, conspicuously attired in a silk Kung Fu suit. He's often pictured with Duterte or

Secretary of Foreign Affairs Perfecto Yasay Jr., the two people that matter most to him to advance China's interests. And if you look at what transpired in the first four months of Digong's presidency, Zhao was pretty darn successful.

Red flags

Former Philippine President Fidel Ramos gestures as he speaks to journalists during a trip to Hong Kong, China after the Hague court's ruling over the maritime dispute in South China Sea, August 9, 2016. REUTERS/Tyrone Siu

Ramos must have sensed that something was afoot after his ice-breaking "unofficial" trip to Hong Kong. He seems to have been sidelined by Duterte's "kitchen cabinet," which is presumably pro-China. About two weeks prior to Digong's China trip, Yasay informed Ramos that his trip to Beijing was cancelled. No reason was given for the cancellation; however, the speculation was that Ramos was an "Amboy" (American Boy), a pejorative for someone who is staunchly pro-American.

A few days before Duterte's China trip, Ramos informed Malacanang that he would not be part of the president's delegation. Communications Secretary Martin Andanar said in a press briefing, "He did not say why he won't join but I believe that it is about giving respect to our current President Rodrigo Duterte." But what else could he have said?

A week after Digong arrived from his China trip, Ramos resigned as special envoy to China. But for whatever official reasons why Ramos quit, it will surprise no one if the real reason for his resignation is that Duterte has become "toxic" – that is, politically hazardous — and has to dissociate and distance himself from him. Ramos, a West Point graduate, a retired Lt. General, hero of the EDSA People Power Revolution, and former president of the Philippines, is undoubtedly pro-American and anti-communist, which would certainly make China's leaders uneasy in dealing with him.

In an article reported in the Asia Times titled, "Has the Philippines blown its South China Sea win?" (November 2, 2016), it said: "The price the archipelago nation has paid — or will pay — for his China pivot is also enormous. Besides economic and military separation from America, the Philippines' long-standing and most important ally, which will likely negatively impact his country in the long-term, if it is materialized, he has made substantial maritime and territorial concessions.

"With such lavish deals agreed with China, coupled with Beijing's claim of its inherent and indisputable sovereignty over most of the South China Sea, its opposition to the arbitration case and Duterte's alienation of the Philippines' key international partners and allies, the prospect that China will comply fully or even partly with the ruling has become unthinkable."

And this raises the question: Did China trick Digong into giving up so much for so little in return? It seems like it.

ooooo

5
Digong was the 'Manchurian Candidate' all along!
Oct. 24, 2016

In Philippine elections, presidential candidates are labeled according to their perceived political persuasion or ideological beliefs. However, political persuasion doesn't really matter in Philippine politics because Filipino politicians change their political affiliations to suit their personal objectives. There are the "Amboys" (American Boys). There are the "balimbings" (political turncoats and opportunists). And there are the "Manchurian Candidates" (secretly aligned with China).

Then Mayor Rodrigo Duterte meets with Chinese Consul General Song Ronghua (left) and his party during their courtesy call at Marco Polo Hotel during the presidential campaign. (Credit: Bing Gonzales)

The Philippines, which is considered pro-American in every meaning of the word, has always been allied with the U.S., politically, economically, militarily, and culturally (there are five million Filipinos living in the U.S.) since she gained independence from Mother America in 1946. But "independence" from America hasn't really been deeply rooted because of the interdependence of the two countries on matters of foreign policy, economics, and national defense, so much so that the Philippine government didn't see the need for a strong navy and air force to defend her sovereignty and territorial integrity.

With three defense agreements that exist between the two countries – Mutual Defense Treaty (MDT), Visiting Forces Agreement (VFA), and Enhanced Defense Cooperation Agreement (EDCA) – the Philippines feels safe knowing that

Uncle Sam would come to her defense against foreign invaders, notably China. And this airtight fusion, which was sealed with the blood of Filipino and American soldiers who fought side by side during World II, has endured to this day. Indeed, a Social Weather Stations (SWS) survey taken recently showed that Filipinos trust America more than China. It's a testament to the strong ties between the two countries.

It is in this regard that pro-American candidates win in elections. To be perceived as anti-American would be a "kiss of death." Take the case of then Vice President Jejomar Binay who was accused of being a "Manchurian Candidate," which might have been a major factor in his defeat.

Extra-judicial killings

Indeed, Duterte might have been the perfect

"Manchurian Candidate." The fact that he belonged to a minor – hardly heard of — political party and whose ideological beliefs are in the fuzzy shades of gray, Duterte marketed himself as a populist crime-fighter, which the people bought hook, line, and sinker.

Never mind that he had been suspected of allegedly masterminding the extra-judicial killings by the notorious "Davao Death Squad" or DDS – which was oftentimes referred to as the "Duterte Death Squad." Never mind that he was once sympathetic to – or part of — the New People's Army (NPA). Never mind that he had admittedly killed a convicted felon for raping and murdering an Australian missionary.

He skillfully – and cleverly — walked a political tightrope, avoiding slipping to the right or left, which if he did might have ended his campaign. He was a Don Quixote riding a motorcycle and carrying an assault rifle. And he threatened to ride a ski jet to the Scarborough Shoal and plant the Philippine flag. People could hear "Digong, Digong, Digong…" like tinnitus ringing in their ears. And they could hardly wait to see the 100,000 dead bodies that he promised to dump into the Manila Bay to fatten the fishes.

Kingmaker

FVR and Digong.

But if there was one person who is credited for making Digong run for president, it was former president Fidel V. Ramos, or FVR as he's often called. While Duterte acknowledged that it was FVR who encouraged him to run, rumor has it that on one of his trips to see Digong in Davao, FVR brought with him a huge bag, which he handed to Digong. Apparently, whatever was in the bag, it convinced him to run. As the old adage says, "Put your money where your mouth is," FVR might have done just that. But of course, it was just tsismis.

But on a more serious tone, FVR criticized Digong in an article he wrote for the Manila Bulletin titled, "Du30's first 100 days – Team Philippines losing." He said: "In the overall assessment by this writer, we find our Team Philippines losing in the first 100 days of Du30's administration – and losing badly. This is a huge disappointment and let-down to many of us."

On U.S.-Philippine relations, FVR – who was a West Point graduate – said: "Equally discombobulating are the mix of 'off-and-on' statements by P. Digong on Philippines-U.S. relations, particularly on security and economic matters." He also criticized Digong for berating U.S. President Barack Obama, U.N. Secretary General Ban Ki-Moon, and terminating RP-U.S. military exercises. "So what gives??" he asked. "Are we throwing away decades of military partnership, tactical proficiency, compatible weaponry, predictable logistics, and soldier-to-soldier camaraderie just like that?? On P. Du30's say – so???"

In a media interview upon his arrival in Beijing last October 18, Duterte said, "The only hope of the Philippines economically, I'll be frank with you, is China." He described his visit as the "defining moment" of his presidency. "Maybe because I'm Chinese," he said.

"America has lost!"

Duterte and his new patron Xi Jinping.

But what surprised the public was what Digong bluntly told Chinese and Philippine business people at a forum in the Great Hall of the People in Beijing on October 20. "In this venue, your honors, in this venue, I announce my separation from the United States," he said. He declared that he had realigned with China, saying: "Both in military, not maybe social, but economics also. America has lost!" Nobody could have been happier than Chinese Vice Premier Zhang Gaoli who was seated a few feet away from Digong at the podium.

The new triumvirate

The new triumvirate: Duterte, Xi, and Piutin.

With $13.5 billion in deals to be signed between China and the Philippines, Duterte couldn't contain his exuberance. He told the audience: "I've realigned myself with your ideological flow and maybe I will also go to Russia to talk to [President Vladimir] Putin and tell him that there are three of us against the world – China, Philippines and Russia. It's the only way." Is this the "new triumvirate" that would create a new world order… or should I say, disorder?

Whatever came to his mind to include his Third-World country in the company of China and Russia against the world, reminds me of someone who once said, "It's like shooting a loose cannon. There is lot of noise, but no substance – and worst of all, no voice."

Indeed, Digong has been trying very hard to amplify his dissatisfaction against the U.S. But the U.S. is not convinced that Digong has the courage to cut loose from Uncle Sam's protective embrace. What is Digong going to do when the Red Dragon starts reclaiming the Scarborough Shoal? What is he going to do when China tows away the old and rusty BRP Sierra Madre that has served as the Philippines' outpost to protect the Ayungin Reef from Chinese reclamation? What is he going to do when China evicts the Filipino settlers on Pag-Asa Island in the Spratly archipelago? What is he going to do when China declares an Air Defense Identification Zone (ADIZ) over the West Philippine Sea? What is he going to do when China declares a 200-mile exclusive economic zone (EEZ) all around the islands, reefs, and rocks in the West Philippine Sea? What is he going to do when China declares the Recto Bank off limits to Philippine oil and gas exploration? And what is he going to do when China claims the Benham Rise as her territory?

In the final analysis, nobody had any inkling that Digong was the "Manchurian Candidate" all along! And with all the hoopla that his pivot to China has created, the people have to look back at his first 100 days in office – just like what FVR did – and ask themselves: Do we want Digong to pursue a China-centric foreign policy at the expense of a century of building mutual trust between the U.S. and the Philippines?

Ooooo

6

Beware the Ides of October

Oct. 16, 2016

The generals of China's People's Liberation Army (PLA) must be texting each other, saying: "Did you hear what Digong was saying these days? LOL." Another general would probably respond, "He's a weakling like Obama. Hahaha… LOLOL." Another one would probably say, "Well, they both can go to hell so we can take their countries… LMAO." And President Xi Jinping would probably say, "And he's willing to give up the Spratly Islands and Scarborough Shoal for a railroad in Mindanao. Well, I think if I asked for Palawan, he'd give it too. Hehehe…" And the generals would all respond, "Long live Xi Dada! Let's get Luzon, too! ROFLMAO."

Chinese President Xi Jinping and his generals.

Well, as most of you probably know, LOL is the acronym for "Laughing Out Loud," LOLOL is for "Lots of Laughing Out Loud," LMAO is for "Laughing My Ass Off," and ROFLAO is for "Rolling On Floor Laughing My Ass Off." These are all Internet slang used in texting messages.

Seriously, we can all make fun of this satirical conversation but it's not ludicrous at all. The question is: What could possibly make the Chinese generals roll on the floor laughing their asses off? The answer is: Duterte surrendering the Philippines' territories in the West Philippines Sea to China.

Picture this: After former President Benigno Aquino III had won the arbitration case against China, the new president Rodrigo "Digong" Duterte was telling everybody that he didn't want to antagonize China and so he ordered that there would be no more patrols beyond the 12-mile boundary. That's tantamount to surrendering the Philippines' sovereignty over her Exclusive Economic Zone (EEZ). He also decided that there would be no more joint military exercises with the U.S. during his presidency. He also told the American Special Forces in Mindanao to leave. He also threatened to distance his country from the U.S., saying he's about to pass "the point of no return" with the U.S. This is a total reversal of the Philippines' victory in the arbitration case against China. Indeed, this is a classic example of the mantra, "To snatch defeat from the jaws of victory."

Red carpet

Chinese President Xi Jinping must really be tickled pink that he invited Digong to visit China this month. Yep, he'd lay out the red carpet for him, treat him to a 20-course State Dinner, bedazzle him with a tour of the Great Wall, and show him the glitz of Shanghai at night. Xi might even show Digong the ghost cities with hundreds of empty high-rise apartment tenements, and tell him, "You see, we can build these for you in your own country to use in rehabilitating the three million drug addicts that you failed to slaughter," which was in reference to what Digong had said not too long: *"Hitler massacred three million Jews ... there's three million drug addicts... I'd be happy to slaughter them."*

It would probably impress Digong so much that he'd offer to give China a 120-year lease on thousands of hectares of prime real estate land to build these rehabilitation centers. Actually, a "mega" drug rehabilitation facility is now being built in a military camp north of Manila. Funded by Huang Rulun, a Chinese philanthropist and real estate developer, the facility will treat up to 10,000 drug addicts. It is being built using 75 shipping containers of materials imported from China, which begs the question: Why can't they build it with local materials and Filipino labor?

The Duterte administration announced that four more "mega" treatment centers would be built. Duterte said that the Chinese have expressed their readiness to help him fight illegal drugs. However, he also criticized China for not doing enough to stop the flow of methamphetamines – or *shabu* – into the Philippines, which makes one wonder: If the smuggling of *shabu* did not happen, would there be a drug addiction problem in the Philippines?

Chinese drug lords

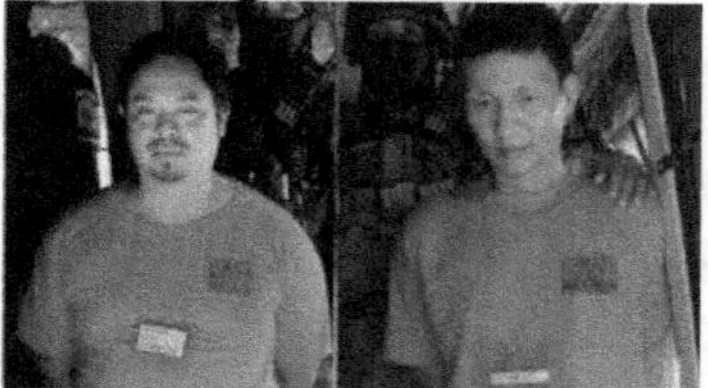

Drug lords Jaybee Sebastian and Wu Tuan (aka Peter Co).

But the bigger problem is not the smuggling of shabu into the Philippines but the presence of Chinese drug lords who have established clandestine laboratories for the production of *shabu* all over the country, one of which was right inside the New Bilibid Prison (NBP) operated by the so-called "Bilibid 19." This group of convicted Chinese drug lords and their Filipino brokers are believed to be operating one of the largest *shabu*laboratories in the country, allegedly with the cooperation of NBP officials and staff.

Buoyed by China's promises of economic and military assistance, Duterte is going to China with an entourage of more than 400 Filipino businessmen – and kibitzers — hoping that they'd benefit from China's "soft power" resources and investments.

But the infusion of Chinese capital into the Philippine economy has a price... a pretty stiff price. To what extent China would give billions – nay, trillions! – in economic aid depends on what concessions Duterte is willing to give to the Chinese. Needless to say, the Chinese would expect more in return for what they would give financially.

While welcoming Chinese investments in the Philippine economy is a wise move by Duterte, but doing it at the expense of American economic and military assistance is not only dangerous, it reduces the geopolitical leverage that the Philippines has to nothing. Zilch... zero!

American protection

Right now, even though the U.S. forces have left, the Philippines is still enjoying the protection provided by the U.S. in three military and defense agreements, to wit: Mutual Defense Treaty (MDT), Visiting Forces Agreement (VFA), and Enhanced Defense Cooperation Agreement (EDCA). They provide the mechanism for the two countries to mobilize and unify their forces to repel or expel invaders. However, it would be a different story if U.S. forces were deployed to the Philippines, which would serve as "tripwire" against invaders.

Take the case of Japan where there are 50,000 U.S. military personnel and hundreds of aircraft and naval units. Likewise with South Korea where 28,000 American troops are stationed in several army and air bases. And just recently, Australia and the U.S. signed an agreement for the deployment of 5,000 American military personnel to Darwin, whose geostrategic location is close to six choke points in and around the Indonesian archipelago, including the heavily used Strait of Malacca.

Surmise it to say, Xi would think twice before he'd invade Japan, South Korea or Australia, simply because of the huge presence of American military forces in those countries. But would Xi hesitate to invade the Philippines? Nah! But wait a minute! Didn't China already invade Philippine territories? Oops!

American withdrawal

US Flag lowered and Philippine flag raised during turnover of Subic Bay Naval Base.

Prior to 1992, when all American bases were kicked out of the Philippines – nobody dared to invade the Philippines. However, two years after the American bases were closed, China occupied the Panganiban (Mischief) Reef and the Philippines couldn't do anything about it simply because she didn't have warships or warplanes to protect her territories. In 2012, China grabbed the Scarborough Shoal and Macclesfield Bank. Two years later, China started building artificial islands on seven reefs and shoals within the Philippines' EEZ. And the latest word is that China would soon reclaim the Scarborough Shoal whose lagoon is as big as the Philippines' capital, Quezon City.

Scarborough Shoal is strategically located in the South China Sea where China could control the South China Sea/West Philippine Sea. It is also in close proximity to the Strait of Luzon, which is the gateway to the Philippine Sea… and beyond.

Ides of October

Supreme Court Senior Associate
Justice Antonio Carpio.

Last October 15, Supreme Court Senior Associate Justice Antonio Carpio voiced his apprehension about losing Scarborough Shoal if Duterte concedes sovereignty over it in exchange for China's economic incentives. He was quoted in a newspaper as saying: *"If Duterte concedes sovereignty, it is a culpable violation of the Constitution, a ground for impeachment."* Then he added: *"But the more important repercussion is, once Duterte concedes sovereignty, we can never recover it because China will never give it back. This is because even if the Philippine Supreme Court voids a possible concession by Duterte, China will not be bound by the ruling of the Philippine Supreme Court."*

Which makes one wonder, was Carpio's message an ominous warning of what could happen or what should be avoided when Duterte meets Xi in Beijing? Beware the Ides of October!

ooooo

7
A Nation in Pain
Oct. 11, 2016

Jennilyn Olayres weeping over the body of her husband, Michael Siaron, who was killed in the Manila metropolitan area. (Reuters)

A Social Weather Stations (SWS) survey conducted last September 24-26 showed Duterte receiving a public satisfaction rating of 76%, "dissatisfied" rating of 11%, and "undecided" rating of 13%. According to SWS, Duterte's +54 "net satisfaction" rating is better than most of his post-EDSA revolution predecessors, except for Fidel V. Ramos who scored +66 in 1992.

During that same period last September, the SWS survey showed that 84% of the respondents are satisfied with the ongoing campaign against illegal drugs, while 8% are dissatisfied and 8% are undecided. The question asked was: "Please tell me how satisfied or dissatisfied you are with the performance of government in its campaign against illegal drugs?"

What SWS survey reveals?

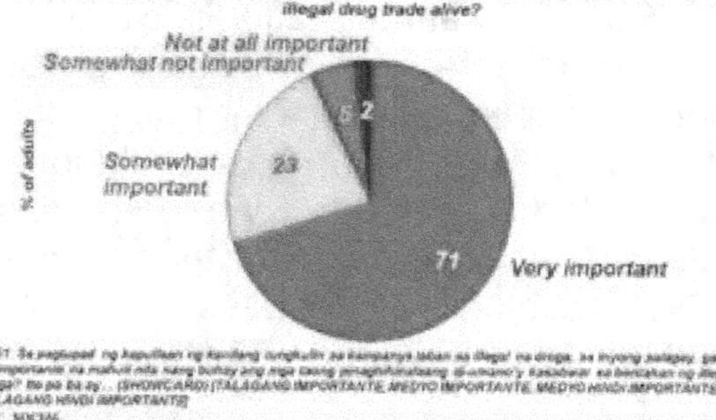

But here is the stinger: 94% of the respondents believed the importance of keeping the drug suspects alive during police operations. Only 6% believed that it was not important. The question asked was: "In the police's fulfillment of their duty in the campaign against illegal drugs, in your opinion, how important is it that they arrest suspects allegedly involved in the illegal drug trade alive?"

Is it then fair to presume that the respondents believed that killing the drug suspects should be avoided and that the police shouldn't be trigger-happy when arresting drug suspects?

It brings to fore the question: Are the police trained to avoid killing the drug suspects whenever possible? Or, is Duterte's "shoot to kill" order encouraging the police officers to use their guns as a "first resort" instead of "last resort."

"Shoot first..."

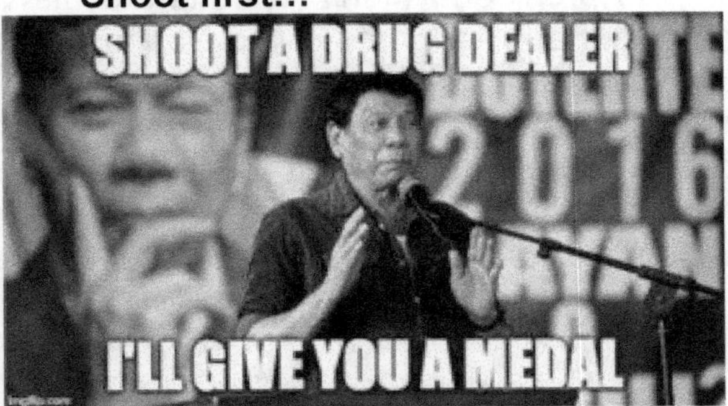

This brings to mind a cliché that's used in police operations, to wit: "Shoot first, ask questions later." Although no police department would openly encourage its policemen to shoot first and ask questions later, there is a culture within the law enforcement community that a policeman should always be ready to shoot first and ask questions later. Their mindset is: It's either they shoot first or they're dead.

However, the "Shoot first, ask questions later" mantra is predicated on a situation where shots weren't meant to kill but merely wound the target so that the police could question him later. But what has been happening is oftentimes the target ends up dead because the police use high-caliber weapons... and at short range. In other words, it's not "Shoot first, ask questions later" but "Shoot to kill." But isn't that in line with what Duterte wants, which is to kill drug pushers and drug addicts? Didn't he say during the campaign, "All of you who are into drugs, you sons of bitches, I will really kill you"? Didn't he offer medals and cash rewards to citizens who killed drug dealers? And few weeks after his oath-taking as president, didn't he reiterate his vow during his inaugural State of the Nation Address (SONA), saying: ""We will not stop until the last drug lord ... and the last pusher have surrendered or are put either behind bars or below the ground, if they so wish"?

Terror effect

Two days before Duterte took his oath, more than 3,000 self-confessed drug pushers and users in South Cotobato and Sultan Kudarat surrendered.

After reaching Duterte's 100th day in office, Communications Secretary Martin Andanar announced in a press conference: *"It's a complete success and the people believe in it. 84% believe in the war against illegal drugs. 700,000 addicts turned themselves in kasama ang (including) 52,000 na drug pushers and drug lords."* He added: *"You see crime dropping. Last July, it dropped at 49%. I don't have it in front of me but I have new data from January to September, crime dropped to about 40 percent."*

While the drop in crime may be attributed to "terror effect" — which was intended against the drug syndicates — it is also terrorizing communities throughout the countries. Citizens are afraid to go out at night lest they be mistaken for drug pushers or users and killed by the police or vigilantes… or people who have an axe to grind against them.

Dutertismo

Former President Fidel V. Ramos confers with President Rodrigo Duterte at the start of the new administration.

In the long run, extra-judicial killings (EJKs) — or "salvaging," a Marcos martial law-era jargon — and other indiscriminate killings would corrode the base of "Dutertismo," a movement based on mass support for Duterte's leadership in fighting corruption, crime, poverty, and other social problems. But, just like similar events in the history of mankind, there is a caveat here. Abuse of power and the impunity of corruption could turn that "mass support" into "mass protest," which could mimic the people power revolutions of the past.

It's interesting to note that one of Duterte's early and ardent supporters – former President Fidel V. Ramos – wrote in his newspaper column: *"In the overall assessment by this writer [Ramos], we find our Team Philippines losing in the first 100 days of Du30's [Duterte] administration – and losing badly. This is a huge disappointment and letdown to many of us."*

"Death under investigation"

"Death under Investigation"

Last September when the SWS survey was taken, the Philippine National Police (PNP) said that 1,011 drug pushers and users were killed from July 1 to September 4. In addition, there were 1,391 deaths considered as "death under investigation" (DUI) or those whose bodies were found with cardboards with the note *"Pusher ako"* (I am a pusher). A month later, the DUIs have increased to 1,745 cases; however, only 321 cases have been filed against the alleged perpetrators – vigilantes? — of the crime, of which 176 cases were considered solved. However, "solved" in PNP parlance doesn't mean the perpetrator has been convicted; it merely means that an arrest has been made.

During a media interview, PNP Director General Ronald "Bato" dela Rosa attributed the deaths of suspected drug pushers to illegal drug syndicates purging their own ranks or due to turf wars or double-crosses in drug transactions. "You will be surprised, this is not the handiwork of vigilantes. These alleged vigilante killings, it turned out, are syndicated killings."

But whether the EJKs were perpetrated by drug syndicates, vigilantes or the police, it is causing international furor because EJKs are considered human rights violations. In particular, U.S. President Barack Obama was concerned about the impunity of EJKs in the Philippines. This did not dwell too well with Duterte, who told Obama, "Go to hell."

The people's "message"

"Stop the killings!"

The Philippines has been getting military and police financial assistance for many years from the U.S. The military receives at least $200 million a year, of which part of it is used in law enforcement. The U.S. military assistance is in jeopardy or it could be terminated to ensure that it will not be used for EJK operations. A U.S. State Department spokesman explained, *"There's a law called the Leahy Law that requires us to routinely and regularly vet security forces that are getting aid and assistance to make sure that any units that violate international law in that regard do not get aid and assistance."*

Indeed, with all the brouhaha over his controversial "War on Drugs," Duterte has become an international pariah. Recently, a French daily newspaper, *"The Liberation,"* in a front-page article, Duterte was described as a "serial killer president." The four-page story also touched on Duterte's expletives against Obama and Pope Francis, and his controversial remarks in which he compared Adolf Hitler's extermination of Jews to his "war on drugs."

At the end of the day, the "message" from the SWS survey last September is crystal clear: While they want Duterte to stop the drug menace, they want him to do it in a way where killings are avoided. "Stop the killings!" was what the people were saying.

The Filipino people are an extraordinary kind of people. They can tolerate the evils of corruption and endure the pains of poverty. But they are too forgiving of others' transgressions. And to the Filipino psyche, killing is never an option.

But in the final analysis, when our nation is in pain, there is only one option and that is, we turn to God – we say, *"Bahala Na."*

oooo

8
'Strategic Diamond' takes shape in the Pacific

Sept. 8, 2016

Obama and Modi: Over a cup of coffee.

With the signing of the Logistics Exchange Memorandum of Agreement (LEMOA) between the U.S. and India, U.S. President Barack Obama achieved a key part of his "Pivot to Asia" strategy. Indeed, it is a major accomplishment considering that the U.S. had been negotiating such an agreement for the past 12 years.

And the beauty of it is while it strengthens the foundation of Obama's rebalancing of U.S. forces in the Indo-Asia-Pacific region, it also reinforces Indian Prime Minister Narendra Modi's Act East policy; thus, extending India's reach beyond the Indian Ocean into the Western

Pacific. What the U.S. and India have accomplished is create a strategic partnership that would be a counterforce to China's aggressive moves in the East and South China Seas and, eventually, the Indian Ocean.

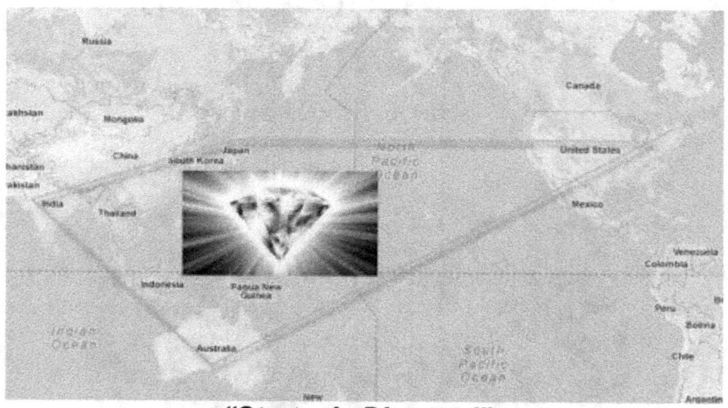

"Strategic Diamond"

In an opinion editorial (op-ed) written by Japanese Prime Minister Shinzo Abe in January 2013, he said that Chinese power is increasingly transfiguring the East and South China Seas into "Lake Beijing." It sounded ominous then. But today, it is pretty close to becoming a reality. China had reclaimed seven reefs in the South China Sea (SCS) and had built artificial islands around them, all within the Exclusive Economic Zone (EEZ) of the Philippines. Recent satellite photos showed that China is building military fortifications including runways, deep-water harbors, lighthouses, and radar installations. And once China declares an Air Defense Identification Zone (ADIZ) over 90% of the SCS that she claims, it would then be nigh impossible to reverse what China did without going to war.

Timetable

Geopolitical and military experts are divided on a timetable. But most of them agree that war between the U.S. and China could happen sooner or later. Some say within a year. Some say 2020, while a few others say 2034.

Evidently, China has put her military modernization plan on the fast tract. While the U.S. still has military advantage, China is fast catching up. And many experts believe that 2020 would be the year when China could surpass the U.S. if the U.S. lets up with her technological edge over China. It is important to note that the Chinese generals have the mindset of Sun Tzu; that is, they wouldn't go to war for as long as they believe the U.S. is stronger than China.

First and Second Island Chains

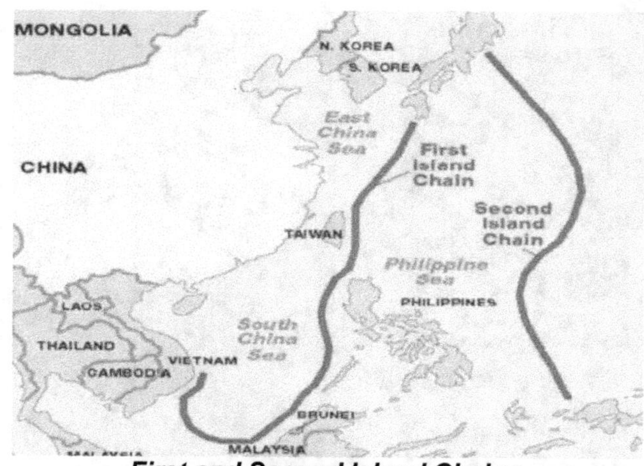

First and Second Island Chains

If you've been following American military strategy since the beginning of the Cold War, she's been busy building military alliance with countries in the Indo-Asia-Pacific region. To date, the U.S. has defense treaties with Japan, South Korea, Taiwan, the Philippines, Thailand, and Australia. These treaty allies – with the exception of the Philippines – are strong militarily, politically, and economically.

While the Philippines may be the weakest link in the First Island Chain – from Japan through Taiwan, the Philippines, Borneo, Malaysia, and Vietnam – it's geostrategic location is a natural barrier against Chinese intrusion into the Second Island Chain –from Japan through Guam, the Marianas Islands, and Papua-New Guinea.

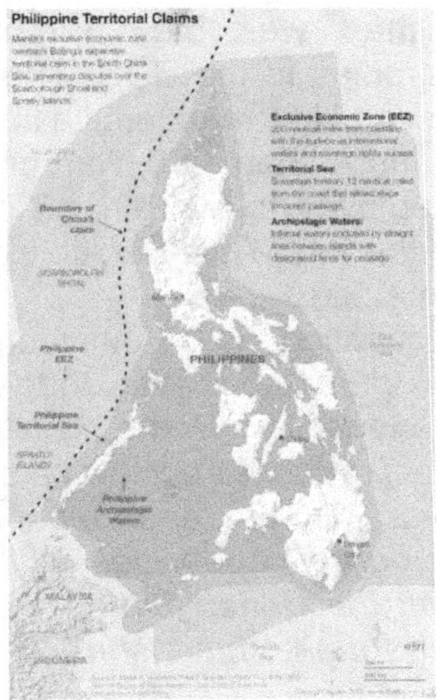

It did not then come as a surprise when the U.S. and the Philippines signed – over the objections of leftists politicians and activists — an Enhanced Defense Cooperation Agreement (EDCA), which is to allow the deployment of American military forces on a "rotational" basis in the country. Right now, four airbases and an army base have been selected to base them. In addition, the U.S. Navy is using the former Subic Bay Naval Base for port calls and to replenish supplies, while American surveillance aircraft are stationed at the former Clark Airbase.

In addition to the six treaty allies, the U.S. has strategic partnership with Singapore, where an American naval flotilla is home ported. The U.S. is also developing defense relationship with Vietnam, while Malaysia and Indonesia aren't too far off the grid. With Malaysia and Indonesia having maritime territorial disputes with China on their own, they welcome the presence of American warships in the SCS. They know that for as long as the U.S. maintains a superior naval presence – more than 200 warships and 400 warplanes deployed to five aircraft carrier strike groups — in the Indo-Asia-Pacific waters, China would be contained.

The question is: How can the U.S. maintain her primacy in the Indo-Asia-Pacific region? The answer is in Prime Minister Abe's op-ed. He said: *"To counteract China's primacy in southern waters [SCS], Japan must augment its combat and police capabilities while forging a 'diamond' with the United States, Australia, and India to defend the commons in East and South Asia."*

Red line

Japanese Prime Minister Shinzo Abe reacts to China's "red line" threat if Japan will join the U.S.-led freedom of navigation operations (FONOPS) in the South China Sea.

The Chinese must have taken note of Abe's op-ed because recently *Kyodo News* reported that China's Ambassador to Japan, Cheng Yonghua, had told a Japanese official that if Japan's Maritime Self-Defense

Force joined the U.S.-led freedom of navigation operations (FONOPS) in the SCS, Japan would have crossed a "red line."

In another diplomatic incident, China warned Australia about a media release pertaining to the Permanent Court of Arbitration (PCA) ruling that favored the Philippines. The media release quoted Australian Foreign Minister Julie Bishop as saying: "The Australian Government calls on the Philippines and China to abide by the ruling, which is final and binding on both parties." Immediately, the Chinese protested against Bishop's "wrong remarks."

Meanwhile, Philippine President Rodrigo Duterte sent former President Fidel V. Ramos to Hong Kong to meet up with some contacts in China. While nothing definitive came out of the meetings, the way is paved for Duterte to initiate bilateral talks with China. China agreed. However, she said that the Philippines mustn't bring the PCA ruling to the table, which raises the question: Would China be willing to give some concessions to the Philippines or would she insists on having it all? But the question is not about keeping those little rocks, reefs, and shoals, it's about who would reign over the entire Indo-Asia-Pacific region?

Chinese Dream

Chinese Admiral Liu Huaqing

In 1982, Chinese Admiral Liu Huaqing, the architect of China's modern naval strategy, was quoted as saying that it would be necessary for China to control the First and Second Island Chains by 2010 and 2020, respectively. "The PLA Navy must be ready to challenge US domination over the Western Pacific and the Indian Ocean in 2040. If China is able to dominate the Second Island Chain seven years from now, the East China Sea will become the backyard of the PLA Navy," he said.

However, China is running behind schedule. But if nobody stops her from reclaiming the Scarborough Shoal, she would be in a position to control the First Island Chain by 2020, the Second Island Chain by 2030, and the Indian Ocean by 2050.

Ultimately, it would all come down to who would be the strongest. But if what Abe had envisioned in 2013 would come to fruition, which is to form a strategic partnership among the four Indo-Asia-Pacific maritime democracies – Japan, U.S., Australia and India — the time may not be too far away for them to challenge any attempt by China to assert total control over the region. Indeed, with the signing of LEMOA, the "strategic diamond" is taking shape in the Indo-Asia-Pacific region.

ooooo

9
Foreign Policy Fiasco
September 19, 2016

Philippine President Rodrigo Duterte, in white, walks away with officials following the ASEAN summit plenary meeting at National Convention Center in Vientiane, Laos, Tuesday, Sept. 6, 2016. (AP Photo/Gemunu Amarasinghe)

It was a very strange week! Was it a full moon... or was it sign of the times? Indeed, a nation's leader going ballistic is not the usual norm even with the likes of... well, I don't want to distract you from the issues so let's move on.

The recent brouhaha on the eve of President Rodrigo Duterte's departure for his first foreign foray to the ASEAN Summit in Vientiane, Laos has left many people wondering what was going on in Duterte's mind? Frankly, a national leader uttering the curse *"putang ina"* – "son of a whore" – to the Pope, the United Nations Secretary General or to the President of the United States, is demeaning the position he holds. And worst, it gives a bad image to the people he leads. And yet, 91% of the Filipino people incredibly hold him in high esteem! As George Takei loves to say, *"Oh my!"*

It all began when Obama, before embarking on his last foreign trip, said that he'd talk to Duterte in Laos about human rights violations. Well, "human rights" is something that apparently hit a raw nerve in "Digong" – Duterte's street moniker – who is reputed to condone killings of illegal drug pushers and users because he said they're not "human beings." Which reminds me of what Digong had told a crowd of cheering admirers, saying he doesn't mind being likened to the late Ugandan dictator Idi Amin, whom human rights activists blamed for the deaths of up to 500,000 people in the 1970s.

Digong and Amin

Duterte and the "Last King of Scotland".

And the similarity between Digong and Amin reminds me of the movie, *"The Last King of Scotland,"* where Amin's mercurial temperament and extreme mood change often makes one wonder if Amin had multiple personalities? Indeed, Duterte once told a group of reporters, *"Ako, palabas-masok ako sa bipolar. One moment seryoso ako, one moment tatapunan ko kayo ng biro."* (I am bipolar. I am serious one moment, and the next moment I will joke with you.)

If true – meaning that he's not joking about suffering from bipolar disorder – then we could be in for a roller coaster ride for the six years of his presidency. Indeed, his underlings – cabinet secretaries and department heads – would be scratching their heads (confused) and wiping their sweating armpits (nervous) every time Digong would give conflicting orders. While they are expected to be compliant and subservient, they would follow Digong's orders, as they understood them, which could lead to bureaucratic chaos. The end result would be a dysfunctional government. But running a government gone berserk is one thing; running amuck around international summitries and gatherings is unspeakably horrible, to say the least.

Digong and Obama

It did not then come as a surprise when Digong bad-mouthed Obama, the leader of the world's most powerful country, before he left for Vientiane to attend the ASEAN meeting. When a reporter asked him how he would explain his administration's recent extrajudicial killings to Obama, he said that Obama must respect him and not just throw questions at him. He then blurted, *"Putang ina*, I will swear at you in that forum!"* And when Obama heard about this, all he said was "He's a colorful guy" and cancelled the meeting. Yep, what Duterte did was like a doberman biting the toe nails of an elephant; it didn't hurt the elephant.

But Digong – a fearless street fighter – has the temerity to admit in front of television in Indonesia that he killed a prisoner who raped an Australian missionary when he was mayor of Davao City. Instantly, the limelight was on him. But is that how a national leader should project himself on the international stage?

While it might have awed some of the leaders attending the summit and treated him like a celebrity, Digong's explosive speech on television had left little doubt that he's someone to be shunned and treated as an international pariah.

One-two-three...

U.S. Special Forces in Mindanao.

But what Digong did in Vientiane was just an appetizer for the media whose voracious appetite for sensational and controversial scandals has no end. And no sooner had Digong landed in Manila than he dropped a bombshell on the U.S. Special Forces fighting the terrorists in Mindanao, saying they "have to go." His reason for their eviction was to keep them from being killed by the Abu Sayyaf terrorist group. The next day — like a one-two-three punch — he announced that joint patrols with the U.S. in the South China Sea would end. He also announced that the Philippines would buy arms from China and Russia, saying that deals are already "in the pipeline." He then disclosed that China had offered to provide him with a personal plane to use. His own "Air Force One"?

The following day, Chinese Vice Foreign Minister Liu Zhenmin welcomed Digong's "independent foreign policy" and remarked that relations between the two countries "are at a new turning point." Not so fast, pal, because the following day, Digong declined the offer saying that the plane might have more problems than him taking commercial flights. And jokingly – or seriously? – he said the plane might explode!

That, in a nutshell, was Digong's maiden "independent foreign policy." Evidently, he didn't consult with his Foreign Affairs Secretary Perfecto Yasay Jr. and National Defense Secretary Delfin Lorenzana to make sure that the independent foreign policy he was pursuing would not put the country in harm's way. But while there is nothing wrong with taking an independent course in foreign affairs, history tells us "Never burn your bridges" because you'd never know when you would need it to go back.

Damage control

A few days later, Yasay flew to Washington DC to meet with U.S. Secretary of State John Kerry to clarify that Duterte's message to the U.S. Special Forces was not an indication of policy shift. He told Kerry, *"We cannot forever be the little brown brothers of America."* Huh? It's amazing that some Filipinos are still using that archaic line.

"We cannot forever be the little brown brothers of America." – Yasay

It must have been excruciatingly painful for Yasay trying to convince Kerry that what looked like a triangle was actually a square. But he didn't realize that Kerry preferred a circle. As someone once said, "Foreign policy is not what it seems." Indeed, what you asked for may not be what you'd get... if you'd get anything at all.

Meanwhile, a few days later, Lorenzana told the House of Representatives' Appropriation Committee that American troops would remain in Mindanao despite the president's statement that he wanted them out of Mindanao. "We still need them there because they have the surveillance capability that our Armed Forces don't have," said Lorenzana, a retired major general. He also told the House committee that the danger of Abu Sayyaf killing or kidnapping the American troops is remotely possible.

Brink of insignificance

While one might presume that the Department of National Defense is in good hands and standing on solid ground, the Department of Foreign Affairs is on shaky ground led by a person whose foreign affairs experience could be categorized as apprentice. And worst, we have President Duterte who has oversized cojones play-acting as Superman, Batman, Iron Man, and Spiderman all rolled into one.

This is not meant to disparage Duterte and Yasay. But the two personify the Republic of the Philippines in the international stage where world leaders see in them the strengths and weaknesses of the country they represent. All it takes is one major foreign policy fiasco to drive the country to the brink of insignificance.

Today, four decades after Idi Amin fled Uganda into exile, many people still vividly see the image of the brutal dictator lording over his ravaged country, which begs the question: Is the Philippines heading the way of Uganda?
(PerryDiaz@gmail.com)

ooooo

10
China Sets Eyes on Benham Rise
September 27, 2016

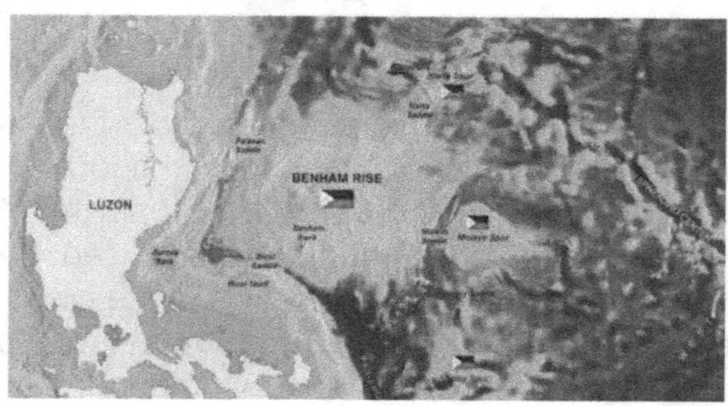

As soon as the United Nations had awarded Benham Rise to the Philippines than China sets her eyes on this undersea landmass in the Philippine Sea. According to the Department of Environment and Natural Resources (DENR), this 13-million-hectare area off the coast of Aurora province is potentially rich in mineral, natural gas deposits, and manganese nodules that are vital in the production of steel. Studies conducted by DENR have also shown large deposits of methane in solid form (methane hydrate or methane ice). Further studies also showed that natural gas deposits in the area would enable the Philippines to achieve energy sufficiency.

The Benham Rise is within the Philippines' exclusive economic zone (EEZ). However, she did not claim it until 2008. The following year, the Philippines, which was the sole claimant, formally submitted her claim to the U. N. Commission on the Limits of the Continental Shelf.

Larger than the entire island of Luzon, Benham Rise was awarded to the Philippines in 2012, after the United Nations approved her claim that Benham Rise was an extension of her continental shelf. In December 2013, the U.N. Convention on the Law of the Sea (UNCLOS) informed the DENR – with finality — that Benham Rise is part of the country's continental shelf and territory. As such, it is not subject to any maritime boundary disputes and claims. Wrong!

In February 2016, the Philippines' Bureau of Fisheries and Aquatic Resources (BFAR) reported that several Chinese ships were seen in the Benham Rise. The following July, China Daily published a report about China's "secret undersea exploration" in the Benham Rise area. The report said that China discovered massive mineral deposits. It also said that the volume of natural gas deposits in the area was at par with what was discovered in the Spratly Islands.

Quid pro quo

Xi Jinping and Rodrigo Duterte (Credit: CNNPH)

With the recent warming up of relations between China and the Philippines under the administration of President Rodrigo Duterte, China has a grand opportunity to solidify her hold on the Spratly Islands and Scarborough Shoal when Duterte visits China in October. It is expected that Chinese President Xi Jinping would shower Duterte – who has shown willingness to put the territorial disputes between the two countries in the back burner – with low-interest loans for infrastructure and economic development projects, and military hardware. But as China had demonstrated in previous *"quid pro quo"* deals with third-world countries, she'd get more than what she bargained for.

Indeed, China's "wish list" could include lucrative economic contracts in the areas of energy, transportation, port management, agriculture, mining, and oil and gas exploration. It wouldn't be surprising if China acquires long-term agreements to use the former American bases – such as the Subic Naval Base and Clark Airbase — as logistical support bases for her growing navy and air force that she needs to project power into the Second Island Chain, which runs from the Ogasawara Islands and Volcano Islands of Japan through Guam and the Marianas to Papua-New Guinea.

If China builds an artificial island on top of Scarborough Shoal (which at 58 square miles is slightly smaller than the area of Quezon City, the capital of the Philippines), she'd be in a position to militarize it. And once militarized – like what she did to the seven artificial islands she built in the Spratlys — she'd be able to control the choke point at the Bashi Channel in the Luzon Strait, which is the gateway to the Philippine Sea... and beyond.

Chinese Dream

Chinese Admiral Liu Hoaqing.

In my column ***"China raises the ante"*** *(July 31, 2013),* I wrote:*"Last June 27, 2013, an intriguing article appeared in the Want China Times titled,* **'China to take Second Island Chain by 2020: analyst.'** *It says: 'Within seven years, China will be able to control the Second Island Chain — a series of island groups that runs north to south from the Japanese archipelago to the Bonin and Marshall islands — now that the PLA Navy commands the nation's first aircraft carrier, according to the Hangzhou-based Qianjiang Evening News.'*

"The article also said: 'In 1982, Admiral Liu Huaqing, the former commander of the PLA Navy

and the mastermind of China's modern naval strategy, said that it would be necessary for China to control the First and Second Island Chains by 2010 and 2020. The PLA Navy must be ready to challenge US domination over the Western Pacific and the Indian Ocean in 2040. If China is able to dominate the Second Island Chain seven years from now, the East China Sea will become the backyard of the PLA Navy.' "

Lake Beijing

"Lake Beijing" bounded by Second Island Chain.

With China's goal of controlling the vast Western Pacific, which includes the East China Sea (ECS), South China Sea (SCS), and the Philippine Sea, the entire Western Pacific would be transformed into "Lake Beijing." The Philippines would be right in the middle of the lake, isolated from the rest of the world. "Lake Beijing" would also encompass the mineral-rich Benham Rise as well.

As things are today, China is behind in her timetable to achieve control over the First Island Chain, which includes the ECS and SCS. However, by militarizing the Spratly archipelago, the Paracel Islands, and Scarborough Shoal,

China would be able to establish a "strategic triangle" formed by these three island groups where China could monitor – and control – all the movements in the SCS. The next step would be to declare an Air Defense Identification Zone (ADIZ) over the entire SCS. With an ADIZ already in place over the disputed Senkaku Islands in the ECS, China would then be ready to break out into the Second Island Chain right up to America's doorsteps, Guam. And the last – and final — step would be to take full control of the choke point at the Strait of Malacca, and eventually… penetrate the Indian Ocean.

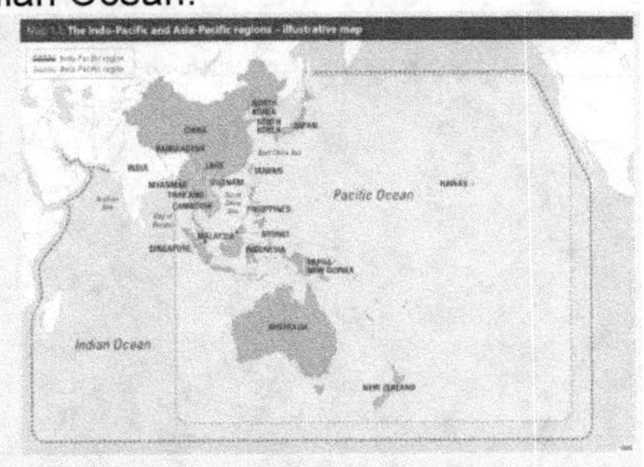

Indo-Asia-Pacific Region.

What is at stake in these disputed waters is control of the huge mineral deposits, marine resources, and the world's busiest maritime lanes. What could the U.S. and her allies in the region do to stop China from gaining control over this huge body of water, which extends more than 10,000 miles from the Indian Ocean to the Second Island Chain?

If the U.S. fails to stop China, she might as well kiss the Indo-Asia-Pacific region goodbye and cocoon herself into isolation just like before she entered World War I. But inaction does not guarantee peace either. The "Munich Appeasement" of 1938 did not stop Germany from invading Czechoslovakia. On the contrary, it emboldened Germany to pursue territorial expansion, thinking that the Great Powers – particularly America — wouldn't intervene. In fact, as Germany continued her conquest of Europe, then U.S. President Franklin Roosevelt told the American people in 1940: "I have said this before, but I shall say it again and again: your boys are not going to be sent into any foreign wars." Wrong!

Iran's Hassan Rouhani, China's Xi Jinping, and Russia's Vladimir Putin.

When Japan attacked Pearl Harbor on December 7, 1941, Roosevelt declared war on Japan the following day. A few days later, Germany declared war on the U.S; thus, bringing the world to war once again for the second time.

North Korea's Kim Jong Un.

Which begs the question: Is appeasement a guarantee for peace or just a momentary stop-gap that would only encourage a rogue country – China, Russia, North Korea or Iran — to start another world war? Sad to say, if history is the barometer of things to come, the imbroglio in the SCS has all the elements of war in the offing. And as China sets her eyes on Benham Rise, the world teeters on the brink of World War III.

ooooo

11
The Philippines at a dangerous crossroads
Oct. 3, 2016

President Rodrigo Duterte's ascension to the Philippine presidency happened at a time when the country was anxiously waiting for the Permanent Court of Arbitration's (PCA) ruling on China's maritime claims in the South China Sea (SCS). And when the ruling was finally released on July 12 invalidating China's "nine-dash line" claim and that China had no historical rights to the rocks, reefs, and shoals in the SCS, the newly installed president found himself in the international limelight. And when the media asked him where he stood in regard to the arbitration case his predecessor former President Benigno S. Aquino initiated, Duterte gave conflicting statements. In a matter of days – nay, hours -- Duterte was pushed into the choppy waters of the SCS to deal with China's aggression.

He found himself in a precarious situation with nobody to call for help. It was sink or swim. And when U.S. President Barack Obama offered to meet with him at the ASEAN Summit in Vientiane, Laos to talk about their countries' security relationship and the issue of human rights violations, Duterte was miffed.

He didn't like Obama saying that he'd like to talk to him about human rights violations. But had he known how U.S. foreign policy works, he would have understood that if he expected the American "sugar daddy" to give the Philippines military assistance, his government would have to pass the litmus test for the preservation of human rights. That was just the way the U.S. Congress would allow the U.S. government to give military assistance to other countries. Instead, just like his "kanto boy" upbringing, Duterte responded the way he was used to, saying: " 'Putang ina,' I will swear at you in that forum." "Putang ina" is the Tagalog phrase for "son of a whore."

For Duterte's outburst, Obama cancelled the meeting. Duterte missed an opportunity to solidify his administration's relationship with the country's only treaty ally and benefactor. **Independent foreign policy** Soon after that incident, which by international standards shouldn't have happened, Duterte started talking about pursuing an "independent foreign policy."

He indicated that he'd ask Russia and China to supply the Philippines with military armaments. He said that he'd open the country to trade with Russia and China; and is prepared to give them 120-year leases. And what would he get in return for prostituting the Philippines to these two countries run by dictators? Oh yeah! Duterte might finally get his railroad in Mindanao. But he should know that whatever economic assistance the Philippines gets from China, China is going to get back huge slices of the Philippines' priceless patrimony.

War against drugs With Duterte's takeover of the government, he pursued to eliminate the drug menace, which according to him has created 4,000 drug pushers and addicts... and counting. He encouraged the national police to go after them and to kill them if they resisted arrest.

And it was at this juncture that Obama was alarmed. Guided by the *Leahy Act,* he wanted to discuss with Duterte the more than 3,000 extrajudicial killings since he took office two months ago. Named after Sen. Patrick Leahy, the law's principal sponsor, *Leahy Act* prohibits the U.S. Department of State and Department of Defense from providing military assistance to foreign military units that violate human rights with impunity. **Gone ballistic** And that's when all hell broke loose! Duterte went ballistic and uttered the "P" word, which is the equivalent of the American "F" word. Duterte then issued – through the media -- a series of policies that would severely affect U.S.-Philippine relations.

In a fit of anger, he declared that he would soon "cross his Rubicon" with the U.S. He also said that the U.S.-Philippine joint military exercises that are now happening would be the last during his presidency. He also said that he would terminate the Philippine Navy's participation with the U.S. in joint patrols in the West Philippine Sea. And, worse, he said that the Philippine Navy would not venture beyond the 12-mile territorial limit, which would be tantamount to surrendering the country's 200-mile exclusive economic zone (EEZ) to China.

If this is the gist of his "independent foreign policy," then what we're seeing here is not independence but a capitulation of national sovereignty, which would undoubtedly lead to vassalage under China. I say this because China will not stop bullying the Philippines Oand other neighboring countries that don't have the ability to defend their sovereignty and territorial integrity.

Simply put, China wants the entire SCS for herself. And she's not coy about it.

Deterrence by denial

Honestly, no country in Asia could defend herself against China's aggressive moves. Even Japan, the world's third largest economic power after the U.S. and China, has to ally herself with the U.S. and allows the U.S. to deploy 50,000 troops on her soil, including several naval and air bases. Ditto with South Korea, who is under constant threat from nuclear-capable North Korea. With several U.S. air bases and 28,000 American troops stationed in her territory, South Koreans feel safer knowing that for as long as the American forces are in their country, North Korean dictator Kim Jong Un would think twice before invading South Korea. Before the American bases were kicked out of the Philippines in 1992, their presence served as deterrence against foreign invasion. The purpose of what is known as "deterrence by denial" is to make aggression difficult and unprofitable by rendering the target harder to take, harder to keep, or both.

To achieve this, the defenders – Filipino forces with the aid of American forces stationed in the Philippines – must be able to inflict substantial damage to the invaders.

Salami-slicing

It's interesting to note that two years after the Americans had left, the Chinese took possession of Panganiban (Mischief) Reef and built fortifications on it. In 2012, China grabbed Scarborough Shoal and prohibited Filipino fisherman from entering its huge lagoon to fish.

Two years after that, China started building artificial islands on seven reefs and shoals – including the Mischief Reef – in the Spratly archipelago, all within the Philippines' EEZ. Thus far, China's unimpeded salami-slicing of Philippine territory has put into question the Philippines' defense capability or the lack thereof. With Duterte's "independent foreign policy" crafted in an atmosphere devoid of reason, the PCA's ruling, which invalidated China's "nine-dash line," is imperiled and the ruling could be deemed moot and academic in light of Duterte's "retreat" from the SCS.

Indeed, the Philippines is not in a position to sever her relationship with the U.S., which Duterte had indicated in his public pronouncements. But his threats to do so are alarmingly dangerous. It doesn't make any sense why he would kowtow to China and Russia at the expense of the U.S., the country's strongest military ally, biggest foreign investor, and second largest export market next to Japan. Unlike communist China, both the Philippines and the U.S. have compatible democratic institutions and both subscribe to the rule of law and adhere to the norms of international order. China doesn't.

In these troubled times, the Philippines has reached a dangerous crossroads where she has to determine which road to take. While it is tempting to try new and uncharted roads, President Duterte should – nay, must! – take the road that would lead the country to economic prosperity and the preservation of individual freedom for her citizens. And if he takes the wrong turn, it could lead to perdition.   ooooo

12
The Philippines' three historical mistake
Sept. 11, 2016

If not for three major mistakes, the Philippines would be strong today – politically, economically, and militarily. We could have taken the place of South Korea as the 11th biggest economic power or even Japan as the third biggest economic power. While Japan and the Philippines were devastated in World War II and South Korea ruined during the Korean War, Japan and South Korea were reborn – like the Phoenix of lore – from the ashes of war. But the Philippines never did. Instead it fell down the economic ladder and became an economic basket case.

In 1966, the Philippines was the second most progressive country in Southeast Asia next to Japan. The ratio of how many times bigger Japan's GDP per capita is against the Philippines was five then. In 1976, the ratio was 13.

The two events that may have contributed to the Philippines' economic decline were the martial law in 1971 and the expiration of the Laurel-Langley Agreement in 1974. It was then that the Philippines came to be known as the "Sick Man of Asia" and stagnated in the company of Third World countries while other Asian countries enjoyed the bounty of what came to be known as "tiger economy."

The Philippines tried to compete with the tiger economies but didn't have the infusion of capital from foreign investors needed to fuel the economy. Thus, the country was hamstrung by lack of capital to build her manufacturing base and generate exportable products just like what the tiger economies were doing.

So why am I saying all these? What was my point? As I postulated earlier, the Philippines could have been at par or better in economic terms with South Korea or even Japan if not for three major mistakes in her history.

First mistake

"I prefer a government run like hell by Filipinos to a government run like heaven by Americans." — Manuel L. Quezon.

The *first mistake* was the premature granting of independence to the Philippines. Through the insistence – and lobbying -- of nationalist Filipino politicians led by Manuel L. Quezon, the United States enacted the Tydings-McDuffie Act in 1934, officially known as the Philippine Independence Act. This Act established the process for the Philippines, then an American colony, to become an independent country after a ten-year period. That would have been in 1945. Tydings-McDuffie also established the Commonwealth of the Philippines, a transitional government prior to independence. Quezon became the president of the Commonwealth. But nobody predicted that the Japanese would invade and occupy the Philippines during World War II.

The Flag of the United States of America is lowered while the Flag of the Philippines is raised during the Independence Day ceremonies on July 4, 1946.

When the war ended in 1945, the ten-year transition as provided by Tydings-McDuffie ended; thus, independence would have been granted. However, due to the devastation suffered by the Philippines, independence was postponed for one year to allow the country to recover. And this is where the *first mistake* occurred. Some political leaders pushed for postponement for five or 10 years to allow for rehabilitation of the country. However, the nationalists insisted on independence right away. They prevailed and independence was granted on July 4, 1946.

Second mistake

December 15, 1954: The Laurel-Langley Agreement is signed, and Senator Jose P. Laurel shakes hands with U.S. Assistant Secretary of State Walter S. Robertson as Chairman James M. Langley smiles in the background.

The *second mistake* was the failure of the Philippines to extend the life of the Laurel-Langley Agreement that amended the Bell Trade Act of 1946, known as the Philippines Trade Act. The Act was designed to set conditions on the Philippine economy and link it to the U.S. economy. The Act also had a provision – known as "parity" clause -- that granted U.S. citizens equal economic rights with Filipinos.

In 1947, the Philippine Constitution was amended to include these parity rights, which was voted by a 78.89% majority in a national plebiscite. Many Filipino politicians supported the Parity Amendment because of the economic benefits it created while the country was recovering from World War II. However, it was controversial among the nationalistic Filipinos because the Philippine Constitution said that the country's natural resources should only be for Filipinos.

In 1955, the Laurel-Langley Agreement was signed. The agreement gave full parity rights to American citizens, business corporations, and investors giving them access to 100% ownership in all areas of the economy. It also made parity privileges reciprocal; thus reducing tariffs on Philippine products exported to the U.S. But the nationalists said that it served foreign interests while exacerbating poverty.

The Agreement expired in 1974 during the Marcos dictatorship. With its expiration, it ended the U.S. authority to control the exchange rate of the Philippine Peso, which was tied at a fixed rate to the U.S. dollar. When the Agreement expired, the exchange rate of the Peso increased drastically. Today, it fluctuates around 45 pesos to the dollar.

And the worst part was the country closed its doors to globalization, which is what countries like Japan, South Korea, and the other tiger economies have embraced. In retrospect, the parity rights may have been the precursor to globalized economy, where trade barriers are systematically removed.

Third mistake

The Senate's "Magnificent 12" raise their clenched fists after winning the vote to reject the extension of the U.S. bases agreement in 1991.

The *third mistake* was the Philippine Senate's rejection of the retention of U.S. bases in the Philippines. In 1991, the Senate voted by a razor-thin majority -- 12-11 -- not to renew the bases agreement. The following year, after attempts were made to keep the bases, the U.S. withdrew all her forces.

US Flag lowered and Philippine flag raised during turnover of Subic Bay Naval Base.

Two years later, China occupied the Panganiban (Mischief) Reef, which was within the Philippines' Exclusive Economic Zone (EEZ). Over the protest of the Philippine government, China built structures on stilts, saying they would be used to shelter fishermen. In 1999, China added more structures, which appeared to look like military fortification.

In 2012, China grabbed Scarborough Shoal and prevented Filipinos from fishing in its environs. A year later, she started building artificial islands around seven rocks and reefs in the Spratly Islands, all within the Philippines' EEZ. Today, satellite photos show runways, harbors, lighthouses, and buildings on these islands. Obviously, China is in the process of militarizing the seven artificial islands.

The question is: If these three historical mistakes did not happen, what would the Philippines be like today?

Had Philippine independence been postponed for 10 years, it would have given the country time and opportunity to recover just like Japan and South Korea did after they were devastated by war. They were smart to put themselves under the military protection of the U.S. and avail of American economic patronage and trade preferences.

Panatag (Scarbor

Meanwhile, with no warships and warplanes, the Philippines was helplessly at the mercy of foreign invaders. Yet, after losing Scarborough Shoal and the Spratlys to China, you'd think that the Philippine leaders are now keen to realize what could be best for the country? It doesn't seem like it. The politicians are still fighting their little turfs among themselves and our national leaders are so protective of the country's sovereignty and national interests from perceived American interference in our internal affairs. But they wouldn't hesitate to remind America of her treaty obligations to defend the Philippines from foreign invasion.

But the challenge the Philippines is facing now is how to avoid making the *fourth mistake*, which is how to deal with China vis-à-vis the territorial disputes in the South China Sea. The Permanent Court of Arbitration's (PCA) ruling that invalidated China's "nine-dash line" claim and has no historical rights to the South China has placed the Philippines in the driver's seat in any bilateral negotiations including pursuing legal action in the international court. Let's not lose that hard-earned legal victory.

While we cannot turn back the wheel of history, we can chart our future by looking back at our history. As someone once said, *"Those who cannot learn from history are doomed to repeat it."*

ooooo

13

Duterte's Honeymoon with China
May 30, 2016

Chinese Ambassador to the Philippines Zhao Jianhua presents President-elect Rodrigo Duterte a copy of the book on Chinese President Xi Jinping. (Office of the City Mayor Davao City via AP)

Like all relationships and marriages, both parties will try to work, or live, harmoniously and reconcile their differences, if any. This is called the "honeymoon" period and it could last for a long time or it can be abbreviated depending on how they relate to each other. It may sound simplistic, but they hope that by the time the honeymoon is over, they'd remain married, partners, allies or friends. Nobody could predict the denouement of their relationships, but as someone once said, "There are no permanent friends or enemies, only permanent interests."

It did not then come as a surprise that America's enemies during World War II – Germany, Japan, Italy – became her allies, and her allies USSR and China became her enemies during the Cold War that followed World War II. And these alliances – North Atlantic Treaty Organization (NATO) and U.S.-Japan Security Treaty – have endured for more than 65 years. And today, NATO has become the bulwark in the defense the 28 NATO countries against enemy invasion, which is crucial to the U.S. national interests.

And in Asia-Pacific, the U.S.-Japan Security Treaty has become a formidable deterrence against Chinese expansionism. Other treaty allies of the U.S. in Asia-Pacific are South Korea, Australia, Taiwan, Thailand, and the Philippines. These alliances form a line of defense along the First Island Chain – linking Japan, Taiwan, Philippines, and Borneo — which would deter China from breaking out into the Western Pacific.

Choke points

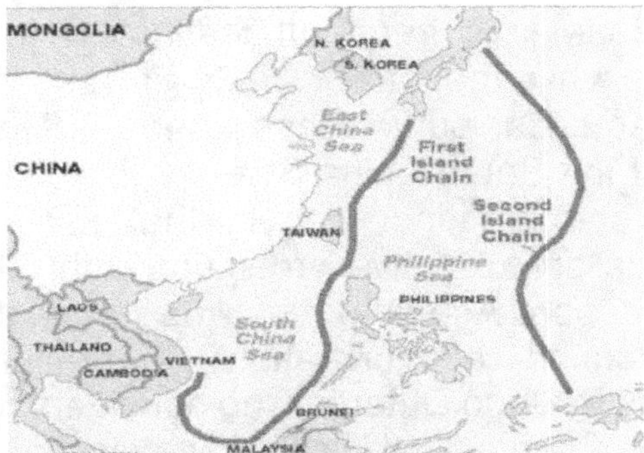

To prevent China from breaking out, the U.S. has to have a strong military presence in Japan and the Philippines, where she can control two major choke points to the Western Pacific. These are the Miyako Strait between Okinawa (Japan) and Taiwan, and the Bashi Channel between Taiwan and the Batanes Islands (Philippines). With several air force bases, a naval base, and 50,000 U.S. troops stationed in Japan, the U.S. maintains strategic dominance over the Miiyako Strait. But it is a different situation in the Bashi Channel, which is wide open and defenseless. However, the U.S. had shown interest in deploying her forces to the Batanes Island and the Laoag City airport in northern Luzon. If the Philippines agrees to this proposal, it would shut off the Bashi Channel from Chinese intrusion... and effectively makes the First Island Chain impenetrable.

Recently, the Philippines and the U.S. agreed on the locations for four American air force units and one army base under the U.S.-Philippines Enhanced Defense Cooperative Agreement (EDCA), which was signed in April 2014. In addition, the former U.S. Subic Bay

Naval Base is a frequent destination for U.S. warships while the former Clark Air Base is used to host American surveillance planes that keep an eye over the South China Sea.

It's interesting to note that EDCA was signed as an executive order under the Aquino administration. As such, it can be terminated by the incoming administration of presumptive president Rodrigo Duterte, who considers himself as a left-of-center politician. However, he admits that he had been on friendly terms with the communist New People's Army (NPA), which makes one wonder: How is he going to deal with China in regard to the territorial disputes in the South China Sea?

Bilateral talks

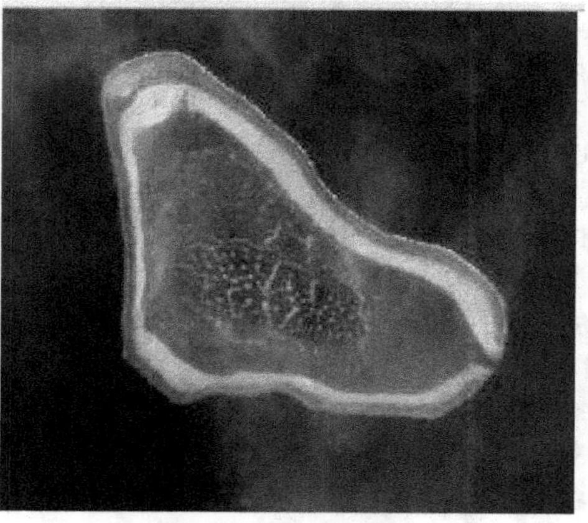

Scarborough Shoal

It is no wonder then that a week after Duterte's landslide victory last May 9, China's ambassador to the Philippines Zhao Jianhua paid him a courtesy call in Davao City. Zhao congratulated him on his victory and expressed his country's expectation of working with his administration to *"properly deal with the differences, deepen traditional friendship, and promote mutually beneficial cooperation, so as to bring the 'bilateral ties' forward."*

Obviously, Zhao was referring to "differences" on the South China Sea territorial disputes, which the Philippines under the Aquino administration had submitted to the United Nations' Permanent Court of Arbitration. It challenged the legality of China's "nine-dash line" claim over the South China Sea under the U.N. Convention on the Law of the Sea (UNCLOS). However, China refused to recognize the authority of the Permanent Court of Arbitration and indicated that she will reject its decision on the matter.

In a recent media interview, Duterte said: *"I told you [referring to China] that is ours, you have no right to be there. And I said whether you believe it or not, that [it] would be the predicate of any further discussions about that territory."*He added, *"At stake is the principle of the law of nations, which says you have the exclusive right to develop and make use of your exclusive economic zone. If there is arbitration, we expect China to follow."*

As Duterte's "honeymoon" with China begins, there would be a lot of posturing by both sides. But the crux of the dispute is China's iron-clad claim to her indisputable sovereignty over the South China Sea demarcated by the "nine-dash line," which has no fixed coordinates simply because it was arbitrarily drawn on a map in 1947 by China's Nationalist government under Chiang Kai Shek. China considers the South China Sea as one of her national core values, which are "non-negotiable."

If Duterte were to initiate bilateral talks with China, he'd be faced with a dilemma. China had in the past offered joint development in the Spratlys. However, she has one pre-condition: That the Philippines concedes to China indisputable sovereignty over the Spratlys. If China sticks to this pre-condition and Duterte accepts it, the Philippines must vacate all the islands she occupies in the Spratlys including the populated Kalayan Island Group (KIG), which is part of Philippine national territory as defined in the Philippine Baselines Law (R.A. No. 3046, as amended by R.A. No. 5446 and R.A. No. 9522) and in Article I of the 1987 Constitution. This would be a violation of the Constitution, which is an impeachable act. Either way, the honeymoon would be over before it started, which begs the question: What would be Duterte's next step?

Junk EDCA?

Chinese facility at Panganiban (Mischief) Reef.

Faced with pressures from militants to scrap EDCA, Mutual Defense Treaty (MDT), Visiting Forces Agreement (VFA), and Logistics Support Agreement (LSA), Duterte will be confronted with the problem of national security. While he had said during the campaign that he was willing to junk EDCA, he is now saying that his administration will continue EDCA since the external defense of the country is weak. Indeed, with no warships and no warplanes to defend her territory, the Philippines would be at the mercy of China.

And once American forces are out of the Philippines – again – what do you expect China would do next? One needs to remember that when the Philippine Senate removed the American bases from Philippine soil in 1992, China took possession of the Panganiban (Mischief) Reef within two years, without firing a shot. With the Spratlys and Scarborough Shoal completely controlled by China, the province of Palawan — which is less than 100 miles from the Spratlys — would be an easy target. China could then claim that the Chinese had been in Palawan since ancient times. And like what she did with the Spratlys, Scarborough Shoal, Paracel Islands (claimed by Vietnam), and Senkaku Islands (claimed by Japan), she would probably come up with another "ancient map" showing Palawan as part of her territories. And pretty soon, the Philippines could become a vassal or client state of China, which would effectively deprive the Filipinos of their sovereignty.

Bully vs. bully

Duterte, street smart – or "kanto boy" — as he is, should know that it takes a bully to fight a bully. He should also be aware that size matters. In other words, a little boy cannot fight a big bully. So what the little boy would do is to call his big brother. In the case of the Philippines, Duterte would turn to big brother America, a bully bigger that China, for help. And this is where EDCA, MDT, VFA, and LSA would level the playing field.

At the end of the day, one might say that Duterte's honeymoon with China would just be an exercise in futility. But the lesson learned would provide him with a clear direction of how – and where — he should lead the country in the next six years.

ooooo

14
Duterte's brand of politics
May 24, 2016

A week after his landslide presidential victory, Rodrigo "Digong" Duterte's cabinet is shaping up: a mixture of business leaders, leftists, communists, political allies, and personal friends. On the surface it looks like a broad-spectrum government reaching out to all sectors of the country. That's good... at least on paper. But at a closer scrutiny, it reveals a master chess player who is lining up his pieces adroitly to achieve *"tunay na pagbabago"* – real change – which he promised during the campaign.

Indeed, Duterte is already raising eyebrows in political circles. While there are the usual skeptics, the reactions are overwhelmingly positive with people hoping that he'd deliver on his promises, which detractors say are impossible to accomplish. But to the common people –

the *masa* – they welcome the radical changes that he vowed to make, which begs the question: Can he deliver? Or are these just promises meant to be broken… just like what traditional politicians – *trapos* – do all the time? But the people have been too forgiving – and forgetful — and continue to elect *trapos* year after year. But this time around, they demonstrated their frustration and anger at the political establishment by voting for a man who admittedly used unorthodox methods, to say it mildly, to rid Davao City of criminality during his term as mayor for two decades.

During a campaign rally, he vowed to kill criminals, saying: "The drug pushers, kidnappers, robbers, find them all and arrest them. If they resist, kill them all." And to emphasize his point, he told the crowd, "Go ahead and charge me with murder, so I could also kill you." At another rally, he promised to "take out" 100,000 criminals and dump them in the Manila Bay so "fish will grow fat." Ordinarily, people would cringe at that kind of vulgarity. But to those who are fed up with the impunity of criminality and corruption, his blunt warnings give them hope that finally there is one fearless leader who was determined to do whatever it would take to protect the people.

Mandate

Indeed, if one has to characterize Duterte's landslide – nay, *tsunami* – victory over his four rivals, it's a protest vote against the corrupt government that the people believed had betrayed the sacred covenant of the EDSA people power revolution 30 years ago. The people see in Duterte someone who has the balls to do the unconventional way to achieve social justice.

While Duterte's overwhelming victory on Election Day may be deemed as a mandate to pursue the things he promised by whatever means he'd chose, there is the danger of failure, which could end his reign as dramatic as his rise to power. He promised early in his campaign that he would eradicate crime and corruption in three to six months, which the people bought hook, line and sinker. They pinned their hopes on this singular promise and expected him to deliver, not a day longer than six months! But what if he failed?

A failure six months into his presidency could wreck his administration beyond repair, just like what happened to his three predecessors, one of which was ousted and another one is currently in detention facing plunder charges, which makes one wonder: Short of declaring martial law, what's his game plan?

Blueprint for success

Recently, he unveiled an 8-point economic agenda. His plan includes: (1) Initiate reforms in tax revenue collections; (2) Set aside 5% of the country's gross domestic product (GDP) for infrastructure spending; (3) Attract foreign investors; (4) Provide support services to farmers to increase productivity, provide irrigation services to them, and promote tourism in rural areas; (5) Address bottlenecks in our land administration and management system; (6) Strengthen basic education system; (7) Improve tax system by indexing tax collection to inflation rate; and (8) Expand and improve implementation of the conditional cash transfer (CCT) program.

It's a good economic plan and it is doable. However, its success hinges on the elimination of corruption. He promised that his administration would vigorously prosecute those who engage in corrupt practices. But isn't this what all his predecessors promised but failed to do? Can he fire and prosecute – no exceptions — his cabinet members and their underlings, most of whom are his political allies or personal friends, if they engage in corruption? Can he stop *jueteng*, which he promised to do, and prosecute the *jueteng* lords who are protected by powerful politicians?

If he has the political will to punish erring subordinates, then he has won half the battle. If so, we should see some of his appointees' heads rolling within six months, because there will always be those who would be tempted by the aphrodisiacal smell of dirty money. If not, he can then kiss his entire promises goodbye and govern the country just like some of his predecessors… that is, corrupt to the core.

It's interesting to note that Duterte has made at least 21 political appointees, most of whom have links to powerful political figures. Ten were appointees or allies of former president Gloria Macapagal-Arroyo, six are Duterte's personal friends or classmates, one is the son of Nacionalista Party stalwart Manny Villar, and four posts are reserved for members of the Communist Party of the Philippines (CPP) under Jose Ma. Sison.

Digong's gambit

Philippines' president-elect Rodrigo Duterte (L) meets China's ambassador to the Philippines Zhao Jianhua during a courtesy call in Davao City / AFP PHOTO / POOL / POOL

And talking of communists, China's ambassador to the Philippines Zhao Jianhua paid Duterte a courtesy call in Davao City on May 16, a day after Duterte said he was open to "bilateral talks" with Beijing over the territorial disputes in the West Philippine Sea (South China Sea). Zhao congratulated Duterte on his victory and expressed his country's expectation of working with Duterte's administration to *"properly deal with the differences, deepen traditional friendship, and promote mutually beneficial cooperation, so as to bring the bilateral ties forward."*

Although Duterte was open to negotiating directly with China, he had made patriotic statements during the campaign about Philippine sovereignty over the disputed territories. To drive his point, he said he would ride a ski jet to the Scarborough Shoal and plant a Philippine flag.

The following day after Zhao's visit, U.S. President Barack Obama called Duterte personally to congratulate him also. Duterte told Obama that he is open to having bilateral talks with China on the disputed territories if the current efforts to resolve the issue failed. However, he assured Obama that the Philippines will continue her mutual interests and is allied with the Western World on the West Philippine Sea row.

During an interview with the media, Duterte said he will hold a steady course on the territorial dispute with China in the West Philippine Sea, and he is in no hurry to quit the multilateral approach pursued by President Benigno Aquino's outgoing administration. He said that if the multilateral approach stalls after two or three years, then he would proceed with bilateral talks. Is this a signal to Obama that if the U.S. cannot stop China in the West Philippine Sea, he'd unilaterally negotiate a settlement with China?

It's noteworthy to mention that during the campaign he suggested that he was willing to set aside the Philippines' claims if China agreed to build railways across the Philippines and hold joint exploration for resources in the disputed waters.

With all these mixed signals, Duterte seems to be playing his cards close to his chest. We can see his opening gambit but nobody knows how he's going to play the end game. And in between his opening gambit and end game, his brand of politics will manifest itself.

Ooooo

15
Duterte: Strongman
With A Soft Spot
May 16, 2016

Some would say that presumptive President-Elect Rodrigo "Rody" or "Digong" Duterte is a leftist, which he admits. Some say he is a communist, which he denies. Others say he is pro-China. And a few say he could be the new "Amboy" – that is, "America's Boy." Honestly, nobody knows that much about his brand of politics.

Who the hell is Digong then? With so many contradictions on what he had said during the campaign, one might say, "This guy is enigmatic!" He's got a little bit of the brashness of Donald Trump—which he denies. "Trump is a racist, I am not," he said. He's got a little bit of the unpredictability of Vladimir Putin. Hmm… He's likened to the benevolent dictator Lee Kuan Yew, which he'd probably say, "Heck, I'm better than

Lee!" Some say he's like the late President Ramon "The Guy" Magsaysay, the most popular president the country ever had. And some see him as a real-life embodiment of the movie character "Dirty Harry." The locals call him "The Punisher" for his zero tolerance against criminals. And what you've got is Trump, Putin, Lee, Magsaysay, and "Dirty Harry" all wrapped into one.

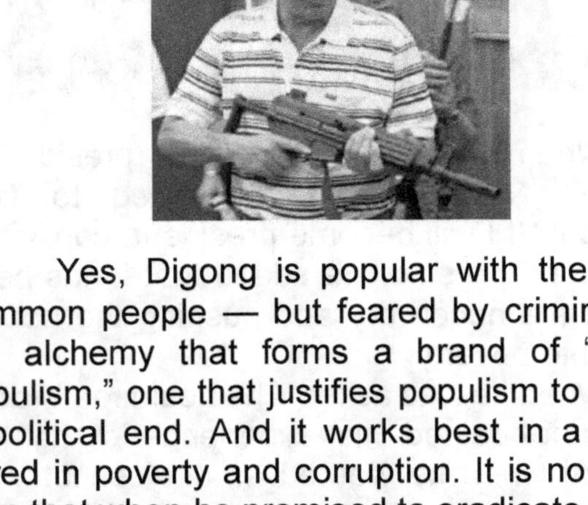

　　　Yes, Digong is popular with the *masa* – common people — but feared by criminals. It's the alchemy that forms a brand of "political populism," one that justifies populism to achieve a political end. And it works best in a country mired in poverty and corruption. It is no wonder then that when he promised to eradicate crime in three to six months, only a few casts doubt that he could do it without declaring martial law, but the majority sees it as flicker of light at the end of a long, dark tunnel. In their minds, if Digong were successful in transforming Davao City from the "Murder Capital of the Philippines" to the safest city in the Philippines and "one of the safest in the world," then that is good enough to give him their votes. Forget that some skeptics don't believe these statistical claims, but when the residents of

Davao City feel safe, then these become "facts" unless proven otherwise. And who among his political rivals have the credibility to challenge his claims?

Fighting corruption

When Duterte entered the presidential race last November, he promised to fight corruption. "If I will become president, corruption has to stop," he said. He added that it has been bleeding the nation dry and pushing the people deeper into poverty.

When he was asked if he could really do it, he said he gained his experience of fighting corruption when he worked as a prosecutor for the *Tanodbayan*, the predecessor of the Ombudsman. He said that he "hounded" the corrupt when he was a *Tanodbayan* prosecutor. "Once upon a time, I was one of only two *Tanodbayan* investigators in Mindanao." With a tinge of populism, he would tell government officials not to shortchange the public. "Don't grab from people's mouth what they are about to eat. What is theirs is theirs," he'd remind them. His passion for the masa gives him credibility that he is capable of fighting corruption.

During the last days of the campaign, Sen. Antonio Trillanes IV dropped a bombshell accusing Duterte of enriching himself while in office. Duterte then opened his bank account to public scrutiny to prove that there was only P17,000 in it, not P211 million as Trillanes had alleged. His quick response added credibility to his character.

By contrast, when Vice President Jejomar Binay, one of his presidential rivals, vowed to fight corruption and go after corrupt officials, nobody believed him. And when asked to disclose his bank accounts, Binay refused. How could the people believe him when he has several plunder charges filed against him before the Office of the Ombudsman, and secretive about his wealth? He has zero credibility.

Economic growth

Not content with outgoing President Benigno Aquino III's economic growth of an average of 6 percent, Duterte plans to pursue a growth of 7-8 percent or higher. "If we want to reduce the poverty rate, we need a higher growth," his spokesman Peter Laviña said. And this begs the question: Can he do it? Yes, he can. However, as what had happened in the administrations of Aquino and his predecessor Gloria Macapagal Arroyo, who have sustained high economic growths, it did not alleviate the suffering of the poor. In spite of the Philippines' high economic growth – it's the "best economy in Southeast Asia today" — poverty and hunger are on the upswing. Why?

In 1973, World Bank president Robert McNamara spoke about poverty, saying: *"Despite a decade of unprecedented increase in the gross national product of the developing countries, the poorest segments of their population have received relatively little benefit [because] rapid growth has been accompanied by greater maldistribution of income in many developing countries." He went on to say that "the growth of GNP is essentially an index of the welfare of the upper income groups. It is quite insensitive to what happens to the poorest 40%, who collectively receive only 10-15% of the total national income."*

It wouldn't take a social scientist or economist a long time to figure out that this was exactly the problem the Philippines faces today, which is: maldistribution of income. Add corruption to the mix and the outcome is: The rich get richer and the poor get poorer. Indeed, if there is one challenge that Duterte will be faced with, it's how he's going to bridge the gap between the rich and the poor? To find the answer, one has to look at our Asian neighbors, the so-called "economic tigers." If there is one measure of their success, it's their growing middle class, which increases as the lower class decreases.

It's noteworthy to mention also that a lot of social scientists are of the opinion that corruption creates poverty, not the other way around. If Duterte makes good of his promise to fight corruption, he'd have a good start in fighting poverty as well. And with his empathy for the poor, Duterte could feel at ease in starting a peaceful political and economic revolution.

Platform for success

Duterte has a three-pronged platform that he plans to implement in the first six months of his presidency, which his spokesman Peter Laviña had outlined as follows:

1. Pursue a 24/7 fight against drugs, criminality, corruption, and poverty;

2. Call on Congress to pass a law for the election of members of a Constitutional Convention to undertake a "major rewriting" of the 1987 Constitution. The objectives are to institute a shift to a federal parliamentary form of government, and to ease the current restrictions on foreign ownership of land, public utilities, educational institutions, and participation in the exploitation of natural resources; and

3. Pursue negotiations and forge peace agreements toward political settlements of the protracted armed conflicts both with the Left revolutionary forces and the Muslim rebel organizations.

One might say that his platform is ambitiously quixotic. But he has one chance to succeed. If he fails, he'd finish his term just like most of his predecessors – mediocre. If he succeeds, he'd be looked upon by generations to come as the Father of the Sixth Philippine Republic. But he can only achieve that if he remains what he is today: a strongman with a soft spot for the *masa*.

ooooo

16
Why I Publish/Reprint Books

Tatay Jobo Elizes
Self-Publisher

Writings are timeless and they act as mirrors to history. I publish writings as they remain relevant anytime. I have seen a lot of good writings in the internet, in magazines and newspapers. But most writers have only one or two articles and therefore not enough material to be published as a book. And yet, many of them need to be published or archived. There are also writers who write a lot but never publish them. There are also old books with no more prints available. The solution is to publish/reprint.

I do this for free because of the print-books-on-demand (POD) system, but the printed or hardcopy is not free

The printed book will always be there among your collections or libraries. Not all use the internet. The internet access has its technical problems. I can produce fiction, non-fiction, in color also.

My booklist can be seen at
http://tinyurl.com/mj76ccq (copy and paste)

Permission had been granted by the author/authors to print their books under my free self-publishing service. They own copyrights to their works.

Interested reader may request free reading of any of my books, articles or essays via online reading or ebook. Just email me.

Thank you.

ooooo